Debbi Fields'
Great American
Desserts

100 Mouthwatering
Easy-to-Prepare Recipes

DEBBI FIELDS

Photography by John Guider

A FIRESIDE BOOK

PUBLISHED BY SIMON & SCHUSTER

New York   London   Toronto   Sydney   Singapore

FIRESIDE
Rockefeller Center
1230 Avenue of the Americas
New York, NY 10020

FIRESIDE and colophon are registered trademarks
of Simon & Schuster, Inc.

Designed by Deborah Kerner

Manufactured in the United States of America

1   3   5   7   9   10   8   6   4   2

The Library of Congress has cataloged the Simon & Schuster
edition as follows:
Fields, Debbi.
[Great American desserts]
Debbi Fields' great American desserts : 100 mouthwatering easy-to-prepare
recipes / Debbi Fields.
p.   cm.
"The companion book to the public television series."
Includes index.
1. Desserts.   2. Cookery, American.   I. Title.
TX773.F52   1996
641.8'6—dc20   96-25748
CIP

ISBN 0-684-83177-5
0-7432-0205-8 (Pbk)

Through my love of baking,
I've been able to share wonderful recipes
as well as a piece of my heart,
especially with my family.

This book is dedicated to my five terrific daughters,
Jessica, Jenessa, Jennifer, Ashley, and McKenzie,
whose love, support, and passion for dessert
always remind me how lucky I am to be a mom.

Acknowledgments

With very special thanks to Sydny Weinberg Miner at Simon & Schuster for her expert guidance; and to Allen Reid and Mady Land of Reid/Land Productions who created the idea for this book and produced the public television series; to Tom Karlo and everyone at KPBS in San Diego; and to the many wonderful people whose efforts and talents made this project happen, especially: the food styling and culinary expertise of Teresa Bucy Blackburn; the recipe development of Michael Lunter; the recipe testing of Kirby Blackburn, Belva Cunningham, Ed Fitzgerald, Judy Fitzgerald, Whitney Kemp, Tonya Marinelli, Alita Miller, Elizabeth Shenk; and the photography by John and Cathy Guider and Blair Morgan. And special appreciation to my collaborator, Evie Righter, for her invaluable literary contributions.

Contents

Great American Desserts
Photographs

Introduction

*G*REAT *AMERICAN DESSERTS* is the fulfillment of a lifelong dream—to share my passion for preparing and enjoying the wonderful variety of American desserts—from simple oatmeal raisin cookies to old-fashioned fruit cobblers to elegant cakes, rich with chocolate and cream.

This love affair began when I was thirteen and started baking in my parents' kitchen in Oakland, California. With five daughters to raise, my mom and dad didn't have a lot of extra money to spend on fancy desserts. So when I attempted to make a traditional American cookie that had chocolate chips in it, I used what was at hand: some margarine, imitation vanilla, fake chocolate chips. I thought I made a pretty good cookie!

It wasn't until about five years later, using my first paycheck, that I went out and bought real butter, pure vanilla, and real chocolate chips—not exactly the things most teenage girls spend their money on! I raced home and made a batch of cookies. It took only one bite for me to understand the importance of what I had done by using the best ingredients. The smiling reaction of family and friends to those fresh-baked cookies encouraged me to pursue my love of baking desserts, and the gift from my heart eventually turned into a business and a career called Mrs. Fields' Cookies. Marriage and five daughters of my own, plus running the company, made for some very hectic but fulfilling years!

Luckily, my family shared my passion for all kinds of sweets and enjoyed helping me in the kitchen as I experimented. Everyone—family and friends—loved apple pie and devil's food cake and cheesecake, brownies and blondies, pan after delicious pan. Not only were the home-made desserts superior to store-bought ones, they turned out to be traditional American favorites, with easy-to-find ingredients available year-round.

After I'd perfected the classic recipes, I did what I've done to every recipe since I ever started cooking: I made them my own. I admit that I'm almost incapable of resisting the temptation to add extra ingredients.

My "extra ingredient" thinking goes a little like this: If classic apple pie is good, why wouldn't a few cranberries make it even better? And instead of a top crust, we could make a lattice

★ ★ ★ *xiii*

crust, for the berries to show through. Or wouldn't it be luscious if macadamia nuts were substituted for the walnuts in brownies? And if people love classic Baked Alaska, with its magical layers of cake and ice cream and meringue, wouldn't your own "Baby" Baked Alaska be even more special?

Which brings me to *Great American Desserts: 100 Mouthwatering, Easy-to-Prepare Recipes.* With each dessert I've interpreted a classic recipe. I've presented a version "à la Debbi," with all the delicious extras it implies.

There are simple recipes, such as shortbreads and bar cookies; elegant cheesecakes; "oldies" but really good "goodies," such as chocolate-filled jelly rolls and fruit pandowdies. For special occasions you can celebrate with a chocolate truffle cake, a chocolate mousse pie, or perfectly poached pears with luxurious sauces. If you want a sweet start to the day, try one of my coffee cakes, muffins, pound cakes, or bundts. There are helpful hints and tips throughout the book to make sure you get the absolutely best results. And by the way, the very best ingredients, pure all the way, are called for throughout.

I'm a working wife and mom, with five daughters and a busy career. Even so, I believe, no matter how busy we are, that gathering around the dinner table with family and friends to share a homecooked meal is important. After twenty years, my husband, Randy, and I still plan family celebrations and get-togethers to make sure we share our important moments. Because of this, I've tried to make the recipes in this book very straightforward. When you can make a step easy for yourself, please do. Use the microwave oven for melting chocolate, the electric mixer for whipping egg whites. The point of dessert, for me, has always been to enjoy it, and that includes the process of making it as well!

I've narrowed down the traditional favorites, which have kept us all together, to share with you. I know you will have as much fun making these recipes as I did. Desserts are a source of unending pleasure. With *Great American Desserts*, there is much here to enjoy, enjoy, enjoy!

Debbi Fields

Part One

Before You Begin

MAKING DESSERTS, ESPECIALLY AMERICAN desserts, has been one of my passionate pastimes for years. I can't think of anything I'd rather make, and I've gotten my whole family involved. It's nothing special for me to wander down to the kitchen and see my daughters getting out the ingredients. Jessica and Jenessa are the cookie queens; Jennifer specializes in brownies; while Ashley and McKenzie are the ingredient tasters and decorators.

For me, it's not only the anticipation of a delicious dessert, something I've made with my own hands and with lots of heart and soul, but the entire process—from selecting what I'm going to make to shopping for the ingredients, and then the really fun part: putting them all together.

No matter how many recipes I've made, I still get excited when a recipe works, when I open the oven door and see a perfectly risen cake or a beautifully browned pie that looks just the way I hoped it would! I've learned over the years, from a lot of trial and error, that there are always ways to bring about your successes. It's called being prepared. First of all, be sure to read the recipe through carefully and to the very end. And equally important, don't start a recipe before organizing your ingredients. Professional cooks have a French term for it—*mise-en-place*—which loosely paraphrased means your ingredients in place. My way of doing this I call my prep tray. Before I begin, I arrange all my ingredients in order of use on a tray, along with whatever measuring utensils I'll need. Once I begin a recipe, I remove the ingredient from the tray as a way of indicating I've added it. With this or a similar system, you can tell at a glance what's in the bowl and what's not. You also know you started off with all the ingredients that were called for. Keeping track of where you are in a recipe is almost impossible if in between steps you're reaching for a spice from one cabinet and removing the sugar canister from another.

Which brings me directly to the types of ingredients I use and want you to, as well. Please make a point of using the best ingredients possible, because by using the best ingredients, you'll get the best results. Now, what do I mean by the "best ingredients"? I mean pure ingredients, no artificial flavors or imitation products. For ingredients such as flour, sugar, baking powder, and soda, where there is little variation in quality, you can use what is readily available where you shop. For the handful of ingredients that follow, though, I have very strong opinions on which ones contribute to the best dessert you can make.

★ *Butter:* Use unsalted butter only, Grade AA, meaning it has scored the highest in quality on a United States Department of Agriculture grading scale for butter. Margarine is not a substitute for butter because it will not provide the same results as pure butter does in either taste or texture when you bake or cook with it. I use unsalted butter to control the amount of salt.

★ *Eggs:* Use the best eggs, graded AA by the USDA, large. Store them in your refrigerator in the carton in which you bought them; they will actually stay fresher than if you put them in the egg tray in your refrigerator.

If you are unsure concerning the freshness of the eggs you're using, there is a quick test to check. Place the egg in front of you on the counter: With your fingertips on either end, gently spin the egg around. If it spins easily, it's still fresh; if it wobbles, going side to side and not around, it should not be used.

★ *Vanilla:* Use pure vanilla extract only. While imitation vanilla flavoring is considerably less expensive than pure vanilla extract, it doesn't have the intensity of flavor that the pure extract does, and were you to buy it, you'd be using much more of it in the long run anyway. Its country of origin is less important to me than the fact that it be pure.

★ *Orange and Lemon Extracts:* Just as there is imitation vanilla flavoring, so there are other imitation extracts. Take the time to find only the pure or natural ones. If your supermarket doesn't carry pure extracts, another good place to look is in your local health-food store.

★ *Chocolate:* There are a lot of chocolate recipes in this book—it's one of my favorite ingredients! To enjoy these desserts to the fullest, you need to buy the best, highest quality, premium chocolate available to you. There are lots of brands, both domestic and European. Avoid any brands that are artificially flavored or with the word "imitation" on the label.

You will find several varieties of pure chocolate: unsweetened (also sometimes called bitter and baking chocolate), which is pure unadulterated chocolate; semisweet (also sometimes called bittersweet), to which some sugar and flavorings have been added; and finally, sweetened, to which more sugar than semisweet and flavorings have been added. The U.S. government has standards that define the amount of chocolate liquor that must be used by chocolate type: Semisweet must contain a minimum of 35 percent liquor; sweetened, a minimum of 29 percent.

Cocoa is pure chocolate liquor from which three-quarters of the cocoa butter has been removed. What remains is then ground into powder. Unsweetened cocoa powder should not be confused with cocoa mixes that have had milk solids and sweeteners added. Cocoa powder contributes color in a baking recipe much more than it does flavor. It's the type of solid chocolate that's called for and how it combines with the other ingredients that determines the ultimate chocolate flavor of a recipe.

Chocolate will keep very well if stored properly. Wrap it tightly in plastic wrap or put it in an airtight container and keep in a cool, dry place where it can remain for as long as one year. "Bloom"—a grayish powdery hue on the surface of the chocolate is a result of the cocoa butter in the chocolate having risen to the surface, and while the chocolate does not look as appealing as it once did, it's still perfectly safe to use and eat.

White chocolate, though technically not chocolate because it doesn't contain chocolate liquor, *must* contain cocoa butter to be considered "real." To find the real kind, you must read the label.

I only use chocolate chips made from real chocolate.

★ *Flour:* I call for all-purpose flour for almost every recipe in this book. Why? One, because all-purpose flour is so readily available, and, two, because its fine texture—which comes from its being a blend of both hard and soft wheats—produces excellent results, whether you're making a tender-crumbed, yellow butter cake for someone's birthday or a flaky pie crust for a Thanksgiving feast. Whether you use bleached or unbleached flour is entirely up to you. They're interchangeable.

Cake flour, made from only soft wheat, is, not surprisingly, softer and silkier than all-purpose flour. I've called for it when the most tender cake crumb is desired. Don't confuse the self-rising variety of cake flour—which has baking powder and salt mixed into it—with regular cake flour. They're not interchangeable.

Be sure to store flour in an airtight container. Sifting all-purpose flour is not necessary, but I do suggest sifting cake flour.

To measure flour, use a dry measuring cup and level the top of the flour off with the back of a straight knife blade. Accuracy, when it comes to flour measurements, matters.

★ *Sugar:* White sugar, brown sugar (both light and dark), and powdered sugar are called for in these pages, and I'm never without a really good supply of each of them at all times! White sugar is just another name for granulated sugar. Brown sugar is white sugar with molasses added. Dark-brown sugar has more molasses than light-brown sugar, producing not only a richer color but also a more pronounced flavor—one reason to think before substituting one for the other. Powdered, or confectioners', sugar is finely ground granulated sugar that has had cornstarch added to it to prevent lumping. Its powdery texture makes it so ideal for dissolving into glazes and frostings, where smoothness counts.

A final word or two about getting the best from your ingredients. Remember that when you bake, you will get the best results if ingredients are at room temperature. About half an hour before starting a recipe, remove the eggs you'll be using from the refrigerator along with the butter and let them come to room temperature. If you need to hasten the warming-up of the eggs, cover them with warm tap water for twenty minutes or so. Do not apply the same thinking to butter, however! It should not be melted in an effort to soften it. Melted butter cannot by definition (being liquid as opposed to solid) function in a batter in the same way softened butter does. It may not always be at the top of your mind when you're baking, but baking is a science, and certain properties cannot be changed if a recipe is to work! For instance, when you melt butter for cookies, it makes the cookies flat, dark, and greasy, rather than light and golden.

Just as ingredients play an incredibly important part in the success of a recipe, so does the equipment you use. I'm sure you already have many of the items below as standard kitchen gear. If you don't have a particular item and don't want to buy it, use a substitute. For example, not everyone has pastry bags fitted with numbered tips. A perfectly acceptable substitute can be fashioned out of a plastic storage bag that you fill, snip off one corner, and squeeze! Making desserts isn't only about cooking, it's also about being creative!

For the desserts in this book, the following amounts to a master list of equipment.

HEAVY-DUTY STANDING ELECTRIC MIXER
HANDHELD ELECTRIC MIXER WITH ROTARY BEATERS
FOOD PROCESSOR
   (OR A BLENDER)

DOUBLE BOILER
   (OR IMPROVISE ONE, BY PLACING A BOWL OVER A SAUCEPAN)
HEAVY-BOTTOMED SAUCEPANS—SMALL, MEDIUM, AND LARGE

LIQUID MEASURING CUPS
NEST OF DRY MEASURING CUPS
MEASURING SPOONS
MIXING BOWLS—SMALL, MEDIUM, AND LARGE
RUBBER SPATULAS—SMALL, MEDIUM, AND LARGE

Metal spatulas—small, medium, and large
Wooden mixing spoons
Wire whisks—small, medium, and balloon

Cake pans—8-inch round, 9-inch round, 8-inch square, 9-inch square
Jelly-roll pan—10 by 15 inches; 12 by 17 inches
Springform pan—9 inches
Aluminum cookie sheets—a minimum of 2
Baking sheets—various sizes
Loaf pan—9 by 5 by 3 inches
Standard 12-cup muffin pan (or two 6-cup muffin pans)
Bundt pan—10 inches, 3-quart capacity
Pie pans—9 inches
Deep-dish pie pans—9 inches
Tart pan with removable bottom—9 inches
Tartlet pans with removable bottoms—4 inches
Baking dishes—9 by 13 inches, 2-quart capacity
Individual heatproof ramekins—1½-cup capacity (or custard cups)

Fine-mesh sieve
Several wire cooling racks

Citrus zester (or a vegetable peeler)
Pastry brush
12-inch polyester pastry bag, fitted with several different tips
Pie weights (or use dried beans or raw rice)
Ice-cream scoop
Melon baller

Baking parchment

With your ingredients and equipment all ready, there's only one thing left to do: Start making some of the great American desserts that follow. Take a batch of brownies to the office; drop off some cookies to a sick friend; or bake a cake just to show appreciation for someone you love.

Part Two

Great American Desserts

Chapter 1

Chocolate Cakes and Layer Cakes

Y OU CANNOT TALK ABOUT great American desserts without talking about cakes because American cooks have created a remarkable number of great cakes since this country was founded. The variety is astonishing! There are layer cakes and pound cakes; butter cakes, sponge cakes, and angel food cakes.

Entire books have been devoted to great cakes. With a chapter, not a book, to work with, I've limited myself to five equally delicious but very different types. It begins with the classic devil's food, dark and rich and tempting. My variation is filled with chocolate cream and covered with an irresistible white chocolate frosting. Tempting doesn't really begin to describe it!

Southern bakers made coconut cake a country-wide favorite. It could be one of the most beautiful cakes ever baked, and so are my two variations on the theme. Carrot cake may be the easiest way I know to get your kids to eat their vegetables! Both my versions, classic and chocolate, share one very important element: a luscious cream cheese frosting.

Before store-bought cakes were common, birthday cakes were homemade, and what made the best birthday cake hands down was a wonderfully light, moist yellow butter cake that took to any icing. My daughters have always chosen their own birthday cakes. Jennifer and Jenessa are both yellow-cake-with-fudge-frosting fans. My version is covered with an irresistible fudge frosting. It's paired with a peaches-and-cream variation that just might be the all-time perfect summer garden party or summer dessert cake. Blended with the right amount of brown sugar, this makes one of my favorites.

I began this chapter with devil's food cake, and I'm ending it with its polar opposite— angel food cake. I've also included a chocolate variation that's as light and airy as the original.

Serve one of these beauties to family and friends, and make any meal a special occasion.

Debbi's Devil's Food Cake

➤ *Makes 12 servings* ◄

Who doesn't love chocolate cake? And when it's the great American classic devil's food cake, I find it even harder to resist. I know it is in our house, especially for Randy. When we were first married, I created my own recipe for him and he was hooked! Now I make it not only every year for his birthday, but many times just to say "you're special."

This devil's food cake is rich and chocolatey and dark and moist. It's made with both cocoa and chocolate, and it has the most wonderful thick chocolate frosting, which I hope you'll use on other cakes as well. I always increase the frosting amounts on my cakes in self-defense! Randy eats his frosting first, then tries everyone else's. The girls keep "testing" while it's being made to be sure it still tastes the same—so it really disappears!

This cake is so easy to make, I'll bet you have all the ingredients already on hand in your cupboard. So, don't wait!

➤ *Equipment Needed:* ★ TWO 9-INCH CAKE PANS ★ ELECTRIC MIXER
★ PASTRY BAG WITH TIP

❖ Cake:

6 ounces semisweet chocolate, coarsely chopped

1¾ cups boiling water

1¼ cups unsweetened cocoa powder

2 cups sifted cake flour (not self-rising, see Tip: Self-rising Flour, page 35)

2 teaspoons baking soda

¼ teaspoon salt

20 tablespoons (2½ sticks) unsalted butter, softened

1¾ cups packed dark brown sugar

4 large eggs, at room temperature

1 tablespoon pure vanilla extract

❖ Frosting:

22 tablespoons (2¾ sticks) unsalted butter, softened

4½ cups sifted powdered sugar

1 cup sifted unsweetened cocoa powder

1 tablespoon pure vanilla extract

¼ cup plus 2 tablespoons milk

1. Preheat the oven to 350 degrees F. Butter both cake pans. Line the bottom of each with a circle of wax paper cut to fit, and butter and flour the paper.

Make the cake layers:

2. Put the chopped chocolate in a heatproof bowl and pour the boiling water over it. Set aside to melt for 5 minutes. Add the cocoa, stir until smooth, and set aside to cool to room temperature.

3. In a small bowl, whisk together the flour, baking soda, and salt.

4. Put the butter and brown sugar in a large bowl and cream together until fluffy, 4 to 5 minutes, using an electric mixer on medium speed. Add the eggs, 1 at a time, beating well after each addition. Scrape down the bowl. Beat in the vanilla. Add the dry ingredients and half of the chocolate mixture and beat to combine. Add the remaining chocolate mixture and beat on low speed until smooth. Use a rubber spatula to scrape down the sides and bottom of the bowl.

5. Divide the batter evenly between the prepared pans and bake for 30 to 40 minutes, or until a cake tester inserted in the centers comes out clean. Remove the cake pans to wire racks and let cool for 10 minutes. Invert the pans onto the racks and let cool completely.

Make the frosting:

6. Put the butter in a large bowl and cream until fluffy using an electric mixer on medium speed.

7. In another large bowl, whisk together the sugar and cocoa; beat one-third of the mixture into the butter. Beat in the vanilla. Add the remaining sugar-cocoa mixture and the milk, beating until the frosting is smooth.

Assemble the cake:

8. Place 1 layer of the cake, rounded side up, on a cake plate and slip strips of wax paper under the edge of the cake to cover the plate. With a metal spatula, generously frost the top. Arrange the remaining layer on top, rounded side up, and frost the sides and finally the top. Remove the wax-paper strips.

9. Fill a pastry bag fitted with a decorative tip with some of the remaining frosting and pipe a border or rosettes or both on the top of the cake.

➤ General Tips for Successful Baking

★ *When you soften your butter, don't let it turn to liquid; this produces a denser cake.*

★ *The more you blend between adding each egg, the more air you add, creating a lighter, moister cake.*

★ *Never forget to preheat your oven!*

★ *Buy an oven thermometer and use it!*

★ *Always bake cakes on the middle rack of the oven unless otherwise specified.*

White Chocolate—Frosted Devil's Food Cake

Why have a two-layer cake when you can have four layers and an opportunity to have twice as much frosting? This special version of devil's food cake is as beautiful to look at as it is to taste.

"Special" describes it, and I like to serve this cake on special occasions such as anniversaries and holidays. To save time, you can make the cake and the fillings in stages ahead of time.

If you're really feeling extravagant—and why not with a cake like this?—serve it with raspberry sauce, which you'll find on page 77. It makes for a beautiful presentation. Drizzle some of the sauce decoratively over each dessert plate and place a slice of the cake on top. Enjoy!

≥ *Equipment Needed:* ★ FOUR 9-INCH CAKE PANS ★ ELECTRIC MIXER

1 recipe Debbi's Devil's Food Cake batter (page 12)

▼ White chocolate frosting:

9 ounces white chocolate, chopped

12 ounces cream cheese, softened

4 tablespoons (½ stick) unsalted butter, softened

2 tablespoons fresh lemon juice

▼ Dark chocolate fudge ganache:

½ cup heavy cream

2 tablespoons unsalted butter

2 ounces semisweet chocolate, finely chopped

2 ounces bittersweet chocolate, finely chopped

▼ Whipped chocolate espresso filling:

½ cup heavy cream

2 teaspoons instant espresso powder

½ teaspoon almond extract

4 ounces semisweet chocolate, finely chopped

❦ Garnish:

Fresh raspberries   Almond slices, toasted (optional)

1. Prepare Debbi's Devil's Food Cake and divide the batter evenly among the 4 prepared cake pans. Bake in a preheated 350-degree F. oven for 15 to 20 minutes, or until a cake tester inserted in the centers comes out clean. Remove the 4 cake pans to wire racks to cool for 10 minutes, then invert the pans and turn the cakes out onto the racks to cool completely.

Make the white chocolate frosting:

2. In the top of a double boiler set over hot, *not* boiling, water on low heat, melt the white chocolate, stirring until smooth. Remove the pan from the heat and cool slightly.

3. Put the cream cheese in a bowl and cream until smooth using the electric mixer on medium speed. Slowly add the cooled white chocolate and beat on low speed until combined. Add the butter and lemon juice and beat until well blended and smooth.

> ### ➤ *Make-Ahead Tips for White* ⬅ *Chocolate—Frosted Devil's Food Cake*
>
> *You can bake the layers in advance. Let the layers cool completely, then wrap individually in plastic wrap, then in foil, and freeze for up to 1 month. Thaw them, with the foil removed but not the plastic wrap, at room temperature.*
>
> *The white chocolate frosting can also be made up to 2 weeks in advance. Cover and store it in the refrigerator. To use, bring to room temperature.*
>
> *The ganache may be made up to 1 week in advance. Store in the refrigerator and bring it to spreading consistency at room temperature before using.*
>
> *The espresso filling can also be made up to 1 week ahead. Keep it well covered in the refrigerator and bring to room temperature before using.*
>
> *If you overbeat the filling and it becomes grainy, don't throw your ingredients away: Spoon the mixture into a small saucepan, remelt it, and chill it again. Beat it a second time, for less time, and everything should be just fine.*

⇛ On Melting Chocolate ⇚

I *love chocolate, and there's a lot of it called for throughout this book. Melting chocolate is easy if you know how, but it must be done carefully.*

When melting chocolate, remember:

★ *Chocolate melts more quickly and evenly when cut into small pieces.*
★ *Moisture causes chocolate to "seize" or clump up. Even the slightest drop can result in an unworkable mass. Should that happen, pour several drops of vegetable oil into it, then stir until smooth. Make sure all the utensils and equipment that come in contact with the chocolate you are about to melt are absolutely clean and dry and never use a wooden spoon, which retains moisture.*
★ *When melting chocolate on the stovetop, you should use a heavy saucepan over low heat. High heat can cause it to seize.*

Make the dark chocolate fudge ganache:

4. In a ceramic or glass bowl covered with plastic wrap, heat the cream, butter, and both chocolates on High in a microwave oven for 30-second intervals, stirring after each interval, until smooth. Cool to room temperature. Refrigerate the ganache until chilled but still of spreading consistency, about 1½ hours.

Make the whipped chocolate espresso filling:

5. In a small saucepan, bring the heavy cream, espresso powder, and almond extract to a low simmer. Remove the pan from the heat and stir in the chocolate until smooth. Pour the mixture into a bowl and chill, stirring occasionally, until cool, about 2 hours. With the electric mixer on medium speed, beat the filling until soft peaks form. Take care not to overbeat.

Assemble the cake:

6. Line the cake plate with strips of wax paper. Place one of the layers, rounded side up, on the plate. Stir the ganache filling, then spread it evenly over the top of the cake.
7. Arrange a second cake layer, rounded side up, and spread it with some of the white chocolate frosting.

How to Melt Chocolate

There are several ways to melt chocolate successfully, and I use all of them depending on how it works with the particular recipe I'm using.

THE STOVETOP METHOD

Place the chopped chocolate in the top of a double boiler or in a bowl set over a pan of barely simmering water. Let the chocolate warm slightly, then stir every minute or so until smooth. Be sure to keep the water at a bare simmer because if it's hotter, boiling or at a rolling boil, it can bubble up and actually splash into the bowl with the chocolate—something you don't want to have happen!

It's also possible to melt chocolate in a heavy saucepan placed directly over the burner. Always use low heat—I can't emphasize that enough. Direct contact increases the possibility of scorching, so pay attention. Keep the heat low, low, low and stir, stir, stir.

THE MICROWAVE METHOD

Place the chopped chocolate in a ceramic or glass bowl, cover the bowl with plastic wrap, and put it in the microwave oven on High for thirty-second intervals, stirring after each interval, until melted. Remove, let stand for a minute or so, and stir until smooth. Microwave ovens are designed differently, of course, and have different heat settings. Adjust the above guidelines to suit your machine.

8. Place the third cake layer on top and spread it with the whipped espresso filling.
9. Place the fourth and last cake layer on top and frost the sides first and then the top of the cake with white chocolate frosting. Remove the wax-paper strips. Garnish the bottom edge of the cake with fresh raspberries. If desired, place more fresh raspberries around the top edge and sprinkle the top with sliced almonds.

Coconut Cake

*O*f southern origin, coconut cake is loved for how beautiful it looks almost as much as for its sweet, tender crumb. Some versions of this cake use milk, but I've used buttermilk—a favorite ingredient of a lot of southern bakers and cooks.

Many a classic coconut cake is covered with a fluffy white frosting made with just sugar, egg whites, and water. I've chosen cream cheese frosting, which is nearly as white and richer by far.

My version of coconut layer cake stands three layers high and uses toasted coconut not only in the frosting but in the actual cake layers as well. Take one bite of the light, moist cake, and you'll become as big a fan as I am.

Equipment Needed: ★ THREE 9-INCH CAKE PANS ★ ELECTRIC MIXER

▼ Cake:

16 tablespoons (2 sticks) unsalted butter, softened

2 cups sugar

1 tablespoon pure vanilla extract

4 large eggs, separated, at room temperature

2 cups all-purpose flour

1 teaspoon baking powder

1 teaspoon baking soda

Pinch of salt

1 cup buttermilk, at room temperature

1 cup shredded sweetened coconut, toasted until golden (see Tip, page 21)

1/4 teaspoon cream of tartar

▼ Frosting:

8 ounces cream cheese, softened

4 tablespoons (1/2 stick) unsalted butter, softened

1 pound powdered sugar

1 cup shredded sweetened coconut, toasted until golden

❦ Garnish:

1½ cups shredded sweetened coconut, toasted until golden

Unsweetened flaked coconut (available in natural foods stores) (optional)

1. Preheat the oven to 350 degrees F. Butter and lightly flour the 3 cake pans.

Make the cake layers:

2. Put the butter and sugar in a large bowl and cream together until fluffy, 4 to 5 minutes, using an electric mixer on medium speed. Add the vanilla and beat until smooth. Add the egg yolks, 1 at a time, beating for 20 seconds after each addition. Scrape down the bowl.

3. In a bowl, whisk together the flour, baking powder, baking soda, and salt. Add the flour mixture to the butter mixture in thirds, alternating with the buttermilk. Beat for 45 seconds after each addition and begin and end with the dry ingredients. Scrape down the bowl. Add the coconut and beat on low speed.

4. In a separate bowl, beat the egg whites until frothy using the electric mixer on high speed. Add the cream of tartar, and beat until stiff peaks form. Fold the beaten whites into the

batter until no white streaks remain. Divide the batter evenly among the 3 prepared pans and smooth the top of each.

5. Bake on the middle rack of the oven for 25 to 30 minutes, or until a toothpick inserted in the centers comes out clean. Remove the pans from the oven to wire racks to cool for 10 minutes. Invert the pans onto the racks and let cool to room temperature.

Make the frosting:

6. Put the cream cheese and butter in a large bowl and beat until smooth using the electric mixer on medium speed. Scrape down the bowl. Beat in the powdered sugar, a little at a time, until creamy and smooth. Scrape down the bowl. With a rubber spatula, gently fold in the toasted coconut and combine well.

Assemble the cake:

7. Place a cake layer on a serving plate with strips of wax paper under the edges and spread the top of it with frosting. Add the second layer and frost the top. Place the remaining layer on top. Frost the sides of the cake, then the top. Garnish by pressing the toasted coconut gently over the top and sides. If desired, place large flakes of coconut over the top. Remove the wax paper.

➤ *Tip:* TOASTING COCONUT

I like to toast coconut until golden, not golden brown, in color. Here's how to do it: Preheat your oven to 325 degrees F. Spread the coconut in an even layer on a baking sheet, then toast it on the top rack of the oven for 10 to 15 minutes, stirring it every 5 minutes to ensure even coloring. Remove, let cool, and use, or store in an airtight container in a cool, dry place.

Lemon-Cream Coconut Cake

⇒ *Makes 12 servings* ⇐

*T*he combination of coconut cake with lemon filling is an old American favorite. From the outside in and the inside out, this moist, sweet cake is filled with the freshness of lemon, enhanced by a touch of fresh lemon peel in the whipped cream frosting.

I think of this as a perfect summer dessert—lemony and light and so very beautiful. One word about preparing this cake for serving: Frost it at the last minute.

⇒ *Equipment Needed:* ★ TWO 9-INCH CAKE PANS ★ ELECTRIC MIXER ★ PASTRY BAG FITTED WITH #6 TIP

❦ Cake:

12 tablespoons (1½ sticks) unsalted butter, softened

2 cups sugar

1 teaspoon pure vanilla extract

1 teaspoon pure lemon extract

2¾ cups all-purpose flour

1 tablespoon baking powder

½ teaspoon salt

4 large egg whites, at room temperature

¼ teaspoon cream of tartar

⅓ cup evaporated milk

3 tablespoons sweetened condensed milk

❦ Lemon filling:

⅔ cup sugar

2 tablespoons cornstarch

1 tablespoon fresh lemon juice

2 egg yolks, at room temperature

1 tablespoon unsalted butter

¾ cup shredded sweetened coconut, toasted until golden brown (see Tip: Toasting Coconut, page 21)

1 teaspoon grated fresh lemon peel (see Tip: Grating Citrus Fruits, page 159)

❦ Lemon whipped cream:

1 cup heavy cream

¼ cup powdered sugar

1 teaspoon fresh lemon juice

1 cup shredded sweetened coconut, toasted until golden   *½ cup sliced almonds, toasted*

1. Preheat the oven to 350 degrees F. Butter and flour the cake pans.

Make the cake layers:

2. Put the butter and sugar in a large bowl and cream until fluffy, 4 to 5 minutes, using the electric mixer on medium speed. Add the vanilla and lemon extracts, and combine well.

3. In another bowl, whisk together the flour, baking powder, and salt. Add the dry ingredients to the butter mixture in thirds, alternating with 1 cup water. Beat for 45 seconds after each addition and begin and end with the dry ingredients. Scrape down the bowl.

4. In a separate bowl, beat the egg whites until frothy using the electric mixer on high speed. Add the cream of tartar and beat until stiff peaks form. Fold the beaten whites gently but thoroughly into the batter. Divide the batter, spooning it evenly between the prepared cake pans and smooth the tops.

5. Bake for 25 to 30 minutes, or until a toothpick inserted in the centers comes out clean. Remove the pans from the oven to wire racks to cool for 10 minutes. Turn the layers out of the pans and let cool on the racks.

6. In a small bowl, combine the evaporated and condensed milks.

7. Using a skewer, poke holes all over the surface of the still-warm cake layers. Drizzle the milk mixture over the tops of both layers and with a pastry brush spread it evenly, letting it soak in. Let the layers cool completely.

Make the lemon filling:

8. In a heavy saucepan whisk together the sugar and cornstarch. Over medium-high heat, stir in the ½ cup water and lemon juice until the mixture is very smooth and bring to a boil, stirring constantly. Lower the heat to maintain a simmer and cook for 2 to 3 minutes, until the mixture thickens and turns glossy. Slowly pour half of the lemon mixture over the egg yolks in a bowl and stir to combine. Pour the egg mixture back into the pan and cook over low heat, stirring constantly, until the mixture begins to "steam" and coats the back of the spoon. Remove the pan from the heat and stir in the butter, coconut, and peel. Let cool to room temperature, stirring occasionally.

Assemble the cake:

9. Place a cake layer on a serving plate with wax paper under the edges and spread the cooled lemon filling over it. Top with the remaining cake layer. Remove the wax paper. Wrap tightly in plastic wrap and chill the cake at least 1 hour, or until ready to serve.

Make the lemon whipped cream:

10. Put the cream, sugar, and lemon juice in a bowl and beat using the electric mixer on medium speed until stiff peaks form. Transfer the cream to the pastry bag and pipe it decoratively over the top of the cake in a wide crisscross pattern. Pipe rosettes around the outer edge of the cake.

11. Sprinkle toasted coconut into the open spaces between the crisscrosses, then stand a sliced almond in each rosette. Serve the cake immediately.

Debbi's German Chocolate Cake

➤ Makes 12 servings ◄

*H*ere's a truly wonderful old-fashioned cake, the kind of recipe handed down from mother to daughter, generation after generation. German Chocolate Cake isn't from Germany, it was named for the person who developed the type of chocolate used in the original recipe. There's a big surprise ingredient here: hot mashed potatoes! If it seems a little funny, stop and think about it for a minute. If sweet potatoes add delicious flavor and texture to a pie or rolls, and cooked potatoes are used in breads, why wouldn't they work in a cake, too? They do!

If you don't want to make potatoes just for this recipe, one night when you're preparing mashed potatoes for your family (before you've seasoned them, of course!), put one cup aside in a container and freeze them. Then when you plan to make this cake, you'll be all set. (*Never* use instant mashed potatoes for this recipe!)

Cooked sugar frostings are a bit tricky to work with because they can go quickly from warm and workable to cool and too hard (literally!) to spread. As soon as the frosting is ready,

assemble this cake. Since the flavor of a chocolate cake improves if made in advance of serving, bake the layers one day and ice them the next.

➤ *Equipment Needed:* ★ THREE 9-INCH CAKE PANS

★ ELECTRIC MIXER

▼ Cake:

8 ounces German's chocolate, chopped and
    divided in half

½ cup boiling water

2 cups all-purpose flour

½ cup unsweetened cocoa powder

1 tablespoon baking powder

1 teaspoon salt

12 tablespoons (1½ sticks) unsalted butter,
    softened

2 cups sugar

1½ teaspoons pure vanilla extract

3 large eggs, separated, at room
    temperature

1 cup hot mashed potatoes

½ cup buttermilk

♥ Coconut pecan frosting:

2¼ cups sugar

18 tablespoons (2¼ sticks) unsalted butter

17 ounces evaporated milk

6 large egg yolks, at room temperature

1 tablespoon plus 1 teaspoon pure vanilla
    extract

3 cups chopped pecans, toasted; divided into 2½
    cups and ½ cup

10½ ounces shredded sweetened coconut, lightly
    toasted, plus additional for garnish (see Tip:
    Toasting Coconut, page 21)

Pecan halves, for garnish

1. Preheat the oven to 350 degrees F. Butter and flour the 3 cake pans.

Make the cake layers:

2. In a ceramic or glass bowl, heat 4 ounces of the chopped chocolate on High in a microwave oven for 30-second intervals, stirring after each interval, until smooth. Set aside
   to cool slightly.

3. In a large bowl, whisk together the flour, cocoa powder, baking powder, and salt.

4. Put the butter and sugar in a large bowl and cream together until fluffy, 4 to 5 minutes,
   using the electric mixer on medium speed. Add the vanilla and beat until combined. Add
   the egg yolks and hot mashed potatoes and beat until combined. Add the melted chocolate
   and combine until blended.

5. Add the dry ingredients to the butter mixture in thirds, alternating with the buttermilk.
   Beat for 45 seconds after each addition, and begin and end with the dry ingredients. Beat
   in the boiling water until smooth. Scrape down the bowl.

6. Beat the egg whites until stiff peaks form using the electric mixer and clean beaters. Fold
   the beaten egg whites into the batter gently but thoroughly with the remaining 4 ounces of
   chopped chocolate. Divide the batter equally among the 3 prepared pans.

7. Bake for 20 to 25 minutes, until a cake tester inserted into the centers comes out with a
   few crumbs on it. Remove the cake pans to wire racks to stand for 10 minutes, then turn
   the cakes out of the pans onto the racks and let cool to room temperature.

Make the coconut pecan frosting:

8. In a large, heavy saucepan over medium heat, combine the sugar, butter, evaporated milk,
   egg yolks, and vanilla. Heat, stirring constantly, about 12 minutes, until the butter is

melted, the sugar is dissolved, and the mixture has turned golden. Remove the pan from the heat, transfer the frosting to a large bowl, and stir in the 2½ cups of pecans and the coconut until well combined. Let the frosting cool, stirring occasionally, until lukewarm and of spreading consistency. (Do not allow the frosting to cool completely, or it will be too thick to spread.)

Assemble the cake:

9. Place a cake layer on a serving plate with wax paper under the edges and spread it with some of the frosting. Add the second cake layer and spread it with some of the frosting. Place the remaining layer on top. Frost the sides and then the top of the cake with the remaining frosting. Remove the wax paper. To decorate the cake, sprinkle the top with toasted coconut, then arrange pecan halves around the outer edge and press the remaining ½ cup of pecans onto the sides.

Carrot Cake

➤ Makes 12 to 16 servings ◄

I like to serve my carrot cake on birthdays—that's how special it is.

This three-layer beauty has several special ingredients that make it super-moist and super-delicious! I use shredded sweet potato and apple and a little crushed pineapple for the sweetness and moisture that the raisins in so many other carrot cake recipes supply. While the batter for this cake may be slightly untraditional, the frosting is not: It's mostly cream cheese and butter, and adds just the right tang and contrast in color to the orangy crumb.

➤ **Equipment Needed:** ★ THREE 9-INCH CAKE PANS
★ ELECTRIC MIXER

❦ Cake:

24 tablespoons (3 sticks) unsalted butter,
softened
1 cup firmly packed light brown sugar
1 cup white sugar
2 teaspoons pure vanilla extract
3 large eggs, at room temperature
2½ cups all-purpose flour
1 teaspoon baking soda
1 teaspoon baking powder
1 teaspoon ground cinnamon
¼ teaspoon salt

½ cup pure apple juice
1½ cups grated peeled carrots (3 or 4
medium)
1 cup shredded peeled sweet potato
(about 1 large)
1 large Granny Smith apple, peeled and
chopped
½ cup crushed pineapple, drained
1 cup coarsely chopped pecans, toasted
3 tablespoons heavy cream

❦ Cream cheese frosting:

16 ounces cream cheese, softened
8 tablespoons (1 stick) unsalted butter, softened
2 teaspoons pure vanilla extract

1 tablespoon fresh lemon juice
2 pounds powdered sugar (see About Powdered
Sugar, page 32)

❦ Garnish:

2 cups chopped pecans, toasted

1. Preheat the oven to 350 degrees F. Butter and flour the 3 cake pans.

Make the cake layers:

2. Put the butter and the brown and white sugars in a large bowl and cream together until fluffy, 4 to 5 minutes, using the electric mixer on medium speed. Scrape down the bowl. Beat in the vanilla. Add the eggs, 1 at a time, beating for 20 seconds after each addition. Scrape down the bowl.

3. In another bowl, whisk together the flour, baking soda, baking powder, cinnamon, and salt. Add the dry ingredients in thirds to the butter mixture, alternating with the apple juice. Beat for 45 seconds after each addition, and begin and end with the flour mixture. Scrape down the bowl. Stir in the carrots, sweet potato, apple, pineapple, and pecans, and blend thoroughly. Divide the batter among the prepared pans and smooth the tops.

4. Bake on the middle rack of the oven for 25 to 30 minutes, or until a toothpick inserted in the centers comes out clean. Remove the cake pans to wire racks to cool for 10 minutes,

then turn them out onto the racks and let cool to room temperature. While the layers are still warm, brush each with 1 tablespoon heavy cream.

Make the cream cheese frosting:

5. Put the cream cheese and butter in a bowl and beat until smooth using the electric mixer on medium speed. Scrape down the bowl. Add the vanilla and lemon juice, and beat until combined. Gradually beat in the sugar on low speed until well blended and smooth.

Assemble the cake:

6. Place a cake layer on a serving plate with wax paper under the edges and spread the top with a thin layer of the frosting. Place a second layer on top and spread it with a thin layer of the frosting. Place the remaining layer on top and frost the sides of the cake. Spread the remaining frosting over the top. Remove the wax paper. Garnish the sides of the cake with the chopped pecans, pressing them gently on with your hands. Refrigerate the cake for 1 hour before serving.

Three-Layer Chocolate Carrot Cake

Makes 12 to 16 servings

What makes this variation on my favorite Carrot Cake (page 27) is the addition of cocoa to a simple batter (no nuts, no apple, and no sweet potato) and lots of coconut in the cream cheese frosting. There's just enough chocolate flavor to be noticeable without being overwhelming and the same moist crumb that distinguishes all great carrot cake.

Equipment Needed:
  ★ THREE 9-INCH CAKE PANS
  ★ ELECTRIC MIXER

❦ Cake:

2 cups all-purpose flour

2 cups sugar

½ cup unsweetened cocoa powder

1 teaspoon baking powder

1 teaspoon baking soda

¼ teaspoon salt

4 large eggs, at room temperature

24 tablespoons (3 sticks) unsalted butter, melted

1 tablespoon pure vanilla extract

2 cups grated peeled carrots (about 4 large)

1 cup crushed pineapple packed in its own juice, undrained

3 tablespoons heavy cream

❦ Coconut cream cheese frosting:

1 recipe Cream Cheese Frosting (page 28)

2 cups shredded sweetened coconut, not toasted

❦ Garnish:

Chopped pecan pieces, toasted

1. Preheat the oven to 350 degrees F. Butter and flour the 3 cake pans.

Make the cake layers:

2. In a large bowl, whisk together the flour, sugar, cocoa, baking powder, baking soda, and salt.

3. Put the eggs, butter, and vanilla in a large bowl and beat until smooth using the electric mixer on medium speed. Add the dry ingredients to the egg mixture and beat until smooth. Beat in the carrots and pineapple until thoroughly blended. Divide the batter among the prepared pans and smooth the tops.

4. Bake on the middle rack of the oven for 30 minutes, or until a toothpick inserted in the centers comes out clean. Remove the cake pans to wire racks and cool for 10 minutes, then turn them out onto the racks and let cool to room temperature. While the layers are still warm, brush with 1 tablespoon heavy cream.

Make the coconut cream cheese frosting:

5. In a bowl, fold the coconut into the cream cheese frosting until thoroughly blended.

Assemble the cake:

6. Layer and frost the cake as directed on page 29, then garnish the top with chopped pecans. Refrigerate the cake for 1 hour before serving.

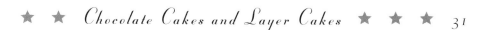

About Powdered Sugar

Powdered sugar, also called confectioners' sugar, is simply finely ground granulated sugar to which cornstarch has been added to prevent it from clumping. It is sold in different degrees of fineness, marked on the box from 4-X to 6-X to 10-X. The higher the number, the finer the sugar will be. It's wonderful for making frostings and icings, and is used in confections where the texture of a grainier sugar would be inappropriate.

If you run out of powdered sugar, remember that you can make your own. In a blender, combine 1 cup granulated sugar and 1 tablespoon cornstarch; blend on medium speed for 2 minutes, until finely ground. Use as you would powdered sugar. You won't ever have to be without it again!

On Checking Baking Powder and Baking Soda

Baking powder and baking soda must be "active" to do what they are meant to do—make a batter rise. Here's how to test them to find out if they are still active.

BAKING POWDER: Put a spoonful of the powder in a cup of hot water; if the water bubbles, the baking powder is active.

BAKING SODA: Put a spoonful of the soda into a cup of vinegar; if the vinegar foams on the top, the soda is active.

A reminder: It's a good idea to replace both your baking powder and baking soda at least every 6 months. Mark the labels with the date they were bought and keep the containers in a cool, dry place. High heat can easily deactivate baking powder.

Rich Yellow Butter Cake
with Fudge Frosting

≽ Makes 12 servings ≼

*H*ere is a wonderful old-fashioned American yellow cake, the kind your grandmother made. I love this recipe for its moist, lovely, tender texture. I've used it for years as the cake for all my daughters' birthday celebrations. It's Jennifer and Jenessa's favorite.

The fudge frosting is incredibly rich and incredibly good. Just be sure not to overbeat it, or it will turn grainy.

A tip about making good cakes in general: Have all your ingredients at room temperature. That way they'll be able to incorporate the maximum amount of air, a must for good texture.

≽ Equipment Needed: ★ TWO 9-INCH CAKE PANS, 2 INCHES DEEP
        ★ ELECTRIC MIXER

❦ Cake:

4 tablespoons (¹/₂ stick) unsalted butter, softened

¹/₂ cup vegetable oil

1¹/₂ cups sugar

6 large egg yolks, at room temperature

1 tablespoon pure vanilla extract

3 cups cake flour, sifted (see Tip, page 35)

1 tablespoon baking powder

1 teaspoon salt

1 cup half-and-half

❦ Fudge frosting:

1¹/₂ pounds semisweet chocolate, chopped into small pieces

2 cups heavy cream

8 tablespoons (1 stick) unsalted butter, in pieces

¹/₂ cup sugar

2 teaspoons pure vanilla extract

1. Preheat the oven to 350 degrees F. Lightly butter and flour the cake pans.

Make the cake layers:

2. Put the butter, vegetable oil, and sugar in a bowl and cream until smooth, 4 to 5 minutes, using the electric mixer on medium speed. Add the egg yolks, 2 at a time, beating for 20 seconds after each addition. Scrape down the bowl. Beat in the vanilla until combined. Scrape down the bowl again.

3. In a large bowl, whisk together the flour, baking powder, and salt. Add the dry ingredients to the butter mixture in thirds, alternating with the half-and-half. Beat for 45 seconds after each addition, and begin and end with the dry ingredients. Scrape down the bowl. Divide the batter between the prepared pans and smooth the surfaces.

4. Bake for 30 to 35 minutes, or until a cake tester inserted in the centers comes out clean. Remove the cake pans to wire racks and let them cool for 10 minutes. Turn the layers out of the pans onto the racks and let cool to room temperature.

Make the Fudge Frosting:

5. Place the chopped chocolate in a large heatproof bowl.
6. In a heavy, medium-size saucepan over medium heat, combine the cream, butter, and sugar. Cook, stirring constantly, until the sugar is dissolved. Increase the heat to medium-high and bring the mixture to a simmer. Immediately pour it over the chocolate. Let stand for 2 minutes, then stir until smooth. Stir in the vanilla. Let the frosting cool for 30 minutes.
7. Set the bowl of frosting in a larger bowl of ice water. Beat the frosting using the electric mixer on medium speed until it thickens and turns lighter in color. (This should take several minutes. The frosting is ready when it no longer runs off the beaters when they are lifted.) Be careful not to overbeat the frosting, or it will turn grainy. Finish by folding the frosting together with a rubber spatula.

Assemble the cake:

8. Place a layer on a cake plate with wax paper under the edges and with a metal spatula spread generously with frosting. Top with the second layer and frost the sides of the cake evenly. Frost the top. Remove the wax paper. If desired, decorate the top of the cake with rosettes or with a shell border.

➤ *Tip:* SELF-RISING FLOUR

Be sure not to use the self-rising variety of cake flour here. You want plain cake flour, which is more finely milled than all-purpose and yields a more tender crumb. Sift as directed because it tends to pack down.

If you've run out of cake flour, here's a substitute. You can still bake this delicious cake with all-purpose flour, adjusting the measurement as follows: Decrease each cup of all-purpose flour by 2 tablespoons and sift twice before using.

Georgia Peach Butter Cake

*I*f Rich Yellow Butter Cake with Fudge Frosting serves as the perfect birthday cake (and it does in our household!), Georgia Peach Butter Cake makes the perfect summer dessert. It's luscious to look at, even better to taste, and it's amazingly light. I have a hard time cutting small slices for myself and friends because they always want seconds. Make it in stages—one day ahead if desired—but assemble it as close to serving time as possible to protect its marvelous combination of textures.

Fresh peaches are the first choice, then frozen. *Never* use canned.

➤ Equipment Needed: ★   9-INCH CAKE PAN   ★   ELECTRIC MIXER
★   PASTRY BAG

❦ Cake:

1¹/₂ cups sifted cake flour

1¹/₂ teaspoons baking powder

¹/₂ teaspoon salt

6 tablespoons (³/₄ stick) unsalted butter, softened

³/₄ cup sugar

2 large eggs, at room temperature

2 tablespoons dark rum

2 teaspoons pure vanilla extract

¹/₂ cup buttermilk

❦ Pastry cream:

²/₃ cup sugar

¹/₄ cup cornstarch

Pinch of salt

2 cups half-and-half

6 large egg yolks, at room temperature

2 tablespoons unsalted butter

1 tablespoon pure vanilla extract

❦ Peaches:

2 pounds peaches, sliced (see Tip, page 38)

³/₄ cup firmly packed light brown sugar

1 tablespoon fresh lemon juice

¹/₄ cup dark rum

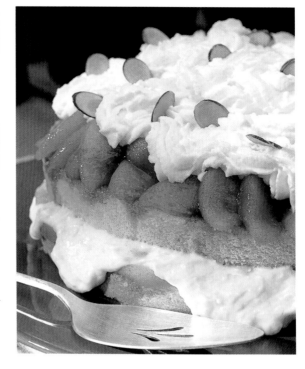

❦ Whipped cream:

1½ cups heavy cream, well chilled
2 tablespoons powdered sugar
2 teaspoons pure vanilla extract

❦ Garnish:

Sliced almonds, lightly toasted (optional)

1. Preheat the oven to 350 degrees F. Butter and flour the cake pan.

Make the cake layers:

2. In a bowl, whisk together the flour, baking powder, and salt.
3. Put the butter and sugar in a large bowl and cream together until fluffy, 4 to 5 minutes, using the electric mixer on medium speed. Scrape down the bowl. Add the eggs, 1 at a time, beating for 20 seconds after each addition. Scrape down the bowl again. Beat in the rum and vanilla. Beat in the flour mixture in thirds, alternating with the buttermilk. Beat for 45 seconds after each addition, and begin and end with the dry ingredients. Scrape down the bowl and beat until smooth. Place the batter in the prepared pan and smooth the top.
4. Bake on the middle rack of the oven for 25 to 30 minutes, or until a toothpick or cake tester inserted in the center comes out clean. Remove the cake pan to a wire rack to cool for 10 minutes, then turn the cake out of the pan onto the rack and let cool to room temperature.

While the cake bakes, make the pastry cream:

5. In a heavy, medium-size saucepan, whisk together the sugar, cornstarch, and salt. Slowly stir in the half-and-half until smooth. Place the pan over medium-high heat and bring the mixture to a boil, stirring constantly. Lower the heat to maintain a simmer and continue cooking for 2 to 3 minutes, stirring constantly.
6. In a bowl, lightly whisk together the egg yolks. Pour half of the hot cream mixture slowly over the egg yolks and whisk to combine. Pour the mixture back into the pan. Cook over low heat, stirring constantly, 3 to 4 minutes, until the cream thickens and just begins to

"steam." Do not let the mixture boil. It should heavily coat the back of the spoon. Stir in the butter and vanilla until combined.

7. Remove the pan from the heat and stir in the butter and vanilla until smooth. Strain through a fine-mesh sieve into a bowl. Cover with plastic wrap directly on the surface to prevent a skin from forming, cool to room temperature, then chill the pastry cream until cold.

Prepare the peaches:

8. In a bowl, toss the peaches with the brown sugar, lemon juice, and rum. Cover and marinate in the refrigerator for up to 1 hour, stirring occasionally.

9. Drain the peaches, reserving the juice. Pour the juice into a small saucepan and reduce over medium-high heat to about ½ cup syrup.

Make the whipped cream:

10. Put the cream, sugar, and vanilla in a chilled bowl and beat until soft peaks form using the electric mixer and chilled beaters.

Assemble the cake:

11. With a serrated knife, carefully cut the cake horizontally in half. Place the bottom layer on a cake plate and brush with half of the peach syrup. Spread all the pastry cream evenly over the cake and top with half of the peaches. Place the remaining cake layer on top, brush with the remaining peach syrup, and top with the remaining peaches.

12. Mound the whipped cream over the peaches and serve immediately. Or for a more decorative touch, with a pastry bag, pipe the whipped cream decoratively over the top of the cake and garnish with sliced almonds, if desired.

➤ *Tip:* PREPARING PEACHES

Use fresh peaches when they're in season. You'll need 2 pounds of ripe ones, and they should be peeled, pitted, and cut into slices ½ inch thick.

To peel the peaches, plunge them one at a time for only a few seconds into a saucepan of boiling water. Remove with a slotted spoon to a bowlful of ice water. The skins should peel right off.

For other times of the year, substitute an equal amount, 2 pounds, of frozen sliced unsweetened peaches, which come in 1-pound bags. Combine them, still frozen, in a bowl with the brown sugar, lemon juice, and rum, and stir to coat. Let marinate as directed, but be sure that the peaches are fully thawed before draining and making the syrup in Step 8.

Debbi's Angel Food Cake

Angel food cake is airy and white and, above all, light. It achieves its dizzying stature because of the ten stiffly beaten egg whites. Beat them with care: Start with whites at room temperature for maximum volume. Use a spanking clean bowl (metal or glass, not plastic) and beat until stiff but not dry. Then fold the flour mixture in gently, with a scooping motion, bringing the whites up and around with the spatula. Be sure not to stir or overmix because overmixing adds too much air to the batter!

I've dressed up this angel food cake with an apricot sauce and a beautiful topping of raspberries. If you're planning to serve the cake soon after finishing it, by all means garnish it as directed with the sauce and the berries on top. If you expect any kind of delay, serve the cake in individual slices, with the sauce and fruit on the side. That way you'll be preserving its divine texture and heavenly color!

In the unlikely event there's any sauce left, you can save it and serve on cheesecake, ice cream, soufflés, or frozen yogurt.

➤ *Equipment Needed:* ★ 10-INCH ANGEL FOOD CAKE PAN WITH A REMOVABLE BOTTOM ★ ELECTRIC MIXER ★ FOOD PROCESSOR WITH METAL BLADE

❦ Angel food cake:

1 cup sifted cake flour

1½ cups sugar, divided into 2 equal measures

¼ teaspoon salt

10 large egg whites, at room temperature

1 teaspoon cream of tartar

2 teaspoons pure vanilla extract

2 teaspoons fresh lemon juice

1½ teaspoons grated fresh lemon peel (see Tip: Grating Citrus Fruits, page 159)

❦ Apricot-orange sauce:

6 ounces dried apricots

1½ cups water

1 cup dry white wine

¾ cup sugar

2 teaspoons pure vanilla extract

½ cup fresh orange juice

❦ Garnish:

Fresh raspberries

1. Preheat the oven to 350 degrees F.

Make the angel food cake:

2. In a bowl, whisk together the flour, ¾ cup sugar, and salt until blended.
3. Put the egg whites in a large metal or glass bowl and beat until frothy using the electric mixer on high speed. Add the cream of tartar and beat until soft peaks form. Slowly add the remaining ¾ cup sugar and beat until shiny, stiff peaks form. With a rubber spatula, fold in the vanilla and lemon juice and peel, and beat until combined.
4. Sift the flour mixture in thirds over the beaten egg whites, folding it in gently but thoroughly.
5. Scrape the batter carefully into the cake pan and run a knife through the batter to release any air bubbles. Bake on the middle rack of the oven for 40 to 45 minutes, or until the top is golden brown and the cake springs back when tested with your finger. Immediately invert the cake pan onto a wire rack and let cool upside down until completely cool. Run the thin blade of a knife around the edges of the pan and remove the cake. Set bottom side up.

Make the apricot-orange sauce:

6. In a heavy, medium-size saucepan, combine the apricots, water, wine, and sugar over medium heat, stirring constantly, until the sugar dissolves. Increase the heat to medium-high and bring to a boil. Turn the heat to low, cover the pan tightly, and simmer for 15 minutes. Remove the pan from the heat and let cool, covered, for 15 minutes. Transfer the mixture to a food processor, add the vanilla, and puree. Add the orange juice, 1 tablespoon at a time, until the desired consistency is reached.

Assemble the cake:

7. Spread a thin layer of the apricot sauce over the top of the cake. Arrange the fresh raspberries on top. Serve the remaining apricot sauce on the side.

Chocolate Angel Food Cake

*A*ngel Food Cake is special, but I do love my chocolate, too. Adding just a touch of cocoa powder turns a beautiful snowy-white angel food cake into a chocolate one. It's light, airy, and elegant. I've added my favorite chocolate sauce as an accompaniment here. Another very good choice is raspberry or even strawberry sauce.

Here's another way to serve this cake that everyone loves. Split the cake in half horizontally, top the bottom layer with the whipped cream, then cover with the remaining layer. Drizzle the chocolate sauce over all or slice and lay each slice in a pool of the sauce. Adding finely grated sweet chocolate to the whipped cream is wonderful, too, and adds still more texture.

☞ *Equipment Needed:* ★ 10-INCH ANGEL FOOD CAKE PAN WITH REMOVABLE BOTTOM ★ ELECTRIC MIXER

❦ Chocolate angel food cake:

1 cup sifted cake flour

1¾ cups sugar, divided into ¾ cup and 1 cup

¼ teaspoon salt

¼ cup plus 1 tablespoon unsweetened cocoa powder

⅓ cup boiling water

1½ teaspoons pure vanilla extract

15 large egg whites, at room temperature (see On Beating Egg Whites, page 104)

1½ teaspoons cream of tartar

❦ Whipped cream:

1 cup heavy cream, well chilled

2 tablespoons powdered sugar

❦ Chocolate sauce:

1 cup heavy cream

8 ounces semisweet chocolate, chopped

1. Preheat the oven to 375 degrees F.

Make the chocolate angel food cake:

2. In a medium-size bowl, whisk together the flour, ¾ cup of the sugar, and the salt until blended.

3. In another bowl, combine the cocoa with the boiling water and stir until blended and smooth. Whisk in the vanilla until combined.

4. With the electric mixer on high speed, in a large, nonplastic bowl, beat the egg whites until frothy. Add the cream of tartar and beat until soft peaks form. Slowly add the remaining 1 cup sugar and beat until shiny, stiff peaks form. Remove 1 cup of the whites and stir into the cocoa mixture until thoroughly blended.

5. Sift the flour mixture, one-quarter at a time, over the beaten egg whites and with a rubber spatula fold the ingredients together gently but thoroughly. Fold the cocoa mixture gently into the egg-white and flour mixture until combined.

6. Scrape the batter into the cake pan and run a knife through the batter to release any air bubbles. Bake the cake on the middle rack of the oven for 40 to 45 minutes, or until the cake springs back when tested with your finger on the top. Immediately invert the cake pan onto a wire rack and let cool upside down until completely cool. Run the thin blade of a knife around the edges of the pan and remove the cake. Set right side up.

Make the whipped cream:
7. With the electric mixer on medium speed and using chilled beaters, in a chilled bowl, beat the cream with the sugar until soft peaks form.

Make the chocolate sauce:
8. In a ceramic or glass bowl covered with plastic wrap, heat the cream with the chocolate on High in a microwave oven for 30-second intervals, stirring after each interval, until smooth.
9. To serve, cut the cake with a serrated knife, arrange each slice on a plate, and drizzle with about 2 tablespoons of the chocolate sauce per serving. Garnish with a dollop of whipped cream.

Chapter 2

Fruit Pies and
Tarts

Depending on how you fashion them, fruit pies and tarts can be plain or fancy, simple or sophisticated, but the pairing of succulent fruit baked in a rich, flaky crust is guaranteed to make mouths water.

I begin this chapter with that most all-American dessert, apple pie! My favorite version is deep-dish strewn with a sweet and crunchy crumb topping and gilded with a little cheddar cheese. It's as easy as, well, apple pie! My more elaborate version of everybody's favorite dessert features a lattice top and an apple filling enhanced by tart, ruby-red cranberries.

Second to apple pie, I confess to loving cherry pie, so I've included an old-fashioned sour cherry pie. Next, I combined chocolate and three kinds of cherries in a one-of-a-kind pie that's as beautiful to look at as it is wonderful to taste.

Fruit tarts are a little more refined than pies. In these tarts, the crust is layered with a creamy filling and topped with luscious fresh fruit. In some tarts, like my Berry Tartlets (page 57), the components of crust, filling, and fruit are prepared separately and put together just before serving. In others, like the Puff Pastry Pear Tart (page 59), the components are assembled and baked together.

No matter how you slice them, these pies and tarts will make you the apple of everybody's eye!

Debbi's Apple Pie

Makes 12 servings

What can possibly be said about apple pie—the symbol of hearth and home and all things American—that hasn't already been said?

Lots! My apple pie is simple, open-faced, deep-dish, and delicious, with a sweet and crunchy oatmeal-walnut crumb topping sprinkled over the fruit. I associate homemade apple pies with friends and family togetherness, warmth and smiles. Bake this pie often when new apples are in, and vary them, combining several varieties at the same time. I called for Golden Delicious because they're my favorite baking apples, are easy to get, and hold up so well when cooked, but you can use your favorite from the many varieties available.

When it comes to making the crust, work it tenderly, for flakiness. It wasn't just the apples that have made apple pie so well loved. A flaky crust plays a very big part.

John Chapman, better known as Johnny Appleseed, may have struck people as being a little odd when he left his native Massachusetts in the late eighteenth century and traveled south and west on foot, planting apple nurseries as he went. Although the Pilgrims brought the apple to this country, without Johnny Appleseed, who knows what pie would have become the symbol of America.

Equipment Needed: ★ 9-INCH DEEP-DISH PIE PAN

❦ Crust:

1½ cups all-purpose flour

¼ teaspoon salt

8 tablespoons (1 stick) cold unsalted butter, cut into chunks

3 to 4 tablespoons ice water

❦ Filling:

5 cups sliced and peeled Golden Delicious apples (about 6 to 8 large apples)

1 cup firmly packed light brown sugar

6 tablespoons cornstarch

1 teaspoon ground cinnamon

¼ teaspoon ground nutmeg

¼ teaspoon salt

♥ Topping:

½ cup quick oats (not instant, see Tip:
    Types of Oats, page 227)
½ cup firmly packed light brown sugar
¼ cup all-purpose flour
3 tablespoons unsalted butter, melted

1 teaspoon pure vanilla extract
½ cup coarsely chopped walnuts

½ cup shredded sharp cheddar cheese, for
    sprinkling

Make the crust:

1. In a bowl, whisk together the flour and salt. With a pastry cutter, cut in the butter until the mixture is coarsely textured with small, irregular flakes and bits the size of small peas. Sprinkle on the ice water, 1 tablespoon at a time, stirring with a fork until the dough just holds together. Gather the dough into a ball, flatten it into a disk, wrap it in plastic wrap, and chill until cold, approximately 1 hour.

2. On a lightly floured surface, roll out the dough into a ⅛-inch-thick round. Transfer the dough to the pie pan and trim and crimp the edges. Put the pan in the freezer for 30 minutes while you prepare the filling.

Make the filling:

3. In a bowl, toss the apples together gently with the brown sugar, cornstarch, cinnamon, nutmeg, and salt until combined.

4. Preheat the oven to 425 degrees F.

Make the topping:

5. In a medium-size bowl, stir together the oats, brown sugar, and flour. Add the butter, vanilla, and walnuts, stirring until well combined. Chill while assembling the pie.

Assemble the pie:

6. Toss the chilled filling before transferring it into the chilled crust. Crumble the chilled topping in pieces evenly over the apples.

7. Bake on the middle rack of the oven for 20 minutes. Lower the oven temperature to 350 degrees F. and bake 25 to 30 minutes more, until the filling is bubbly and the topping lightly brown. Remove the pie pan from the oven to a wire rack, sprinkle evenly with the shredded cheddar, then cool on the wire rack for 1 hour.

8. Serve the pie warm, chilled, or at room temperature.

Lattice-Topped Apple-Cranberry Pie

⇒ *Makes 12 servings* ⇐

*T*his pie combines apples with a truly native American fruit, the cranberry—that beautiful tart red berry associated with New England. The lattice-top design allows the fabulous colors of the cranberries to show through, and the fruit flavors complement the wonderfully flaky crust.

If the over/under weaving of lattice-top strips is new to you, you can still make a latticework top: Lay one layer of strips across the top of the pie, then top with the second layer of strips, placing them at right angles to the first. This is called a "false lattice," but it looks very pretty nonetheless. (And it's done a lot!) If a strip breaks, put it back together with a dab of water, pressing with your fingertips. If you can, work in a cool kitchen and always start with chilled strips. Thin strips of dough are easier to handle if they're cold.

I've called for tart Granny Smith apples here because they're combined with a sour cream–brown sugar filling. Using a Golden Delicious apple, for example, would make the filling too sweet.

⇒ *Equipment Needed:* ★ 9-INCH DEEP-DISH PIE PAN

₩ Crust:

2½ cups all-purpose flour

2 tablespoons sugar

1 teaspoon finely grated fresh orange peel, (see Tip: Grating Citrus Fruits, page 159)

¼ teaspoon salt

16 tablespoons (2 sticks) cold unsalted butter, cut into chunks

6 to 8 tablespoons cold pure apple juice

₩ Filling:

7 to 8 medium Granny Smith apples, peeled, cored, and cut into slices (about 3 pounds)

1 cup cranberries, fresh or frozen, unsweetened

6 tablespoons cornstarch

½ cup firmly packed light brown sugar

½ teaspoon ground nutmeg

½ teaspoon salt

¼ cup sour cream

3 large egg yolks, at room temperature

2 tablespoons honey

1 teaspoon pure vanilla extract

♥ Topping:

½ cup chopped pecans

½ cup quick oats (not instant, see Tip: Types of Oats, page 227)

½ cup firmly packed light brown sugar

1 tablespoon ground cinnamon

4 tablespoons (½ stick) unsalted butter, melted

♥ Eggwash

1 large egg, lightly beaten

2 teaspoons sugar

Make the crust:

1. In a bowl, whisk together the flour, sugar, orange peel, and salt. With a pastry cutter, cut in the butter until the mixture is coarsely textured with small, irregular flakes and bits the size of small peas. With a fork, stir in the apple juice, 1 tablespoon at a time, until the dough can be gathered into a ball. Flatten the dough ball into a disk, wrap it in plastic wrap, and chill for 1 hour.

Make the filling:

2. In a large bowl, toss the apples and cranberries with the cornstarch, brown sugar, nutmeg, and salt until combined.

3. In a separate bowl, stir together the sour cream, egg yolks, honey, and vanilla until smooth. Pour over the apples and fold to combine.

4. Preheat the oven to 425 degrees F.

5. On a lightly floured surface, roll half of the dough out into a ⅛-inch-thick round and at least 1 inch larger than the pie pan. Transfer the dough to the pie pan and trim the edges slightly. Chill in the freezer while preparing the topping.

Make the topping:

6. In a small bowl, stir together the pecans, oats, sugar, and cinnamon. Stir in the melted butter until thoroughly combined.

Assemble the pie:

7. Stir the apple filling again before transferring it into the chilled pie shell. Crumble the nut topping evenly over the filling.

8. On a lightly floured surface, roll out the remaining dough into a ⅛-inch-thick round and cut it into ½-inch-wide strips. Place the strips in a lattice pattern over the filling, folding over the edges of the bottom crust to seal the strips. Crimp the outer rim decoratively with your fingertips.

9. Brush the lattice strips lightly with the eggwash.

10. Bake on the middle rack of the oven for 20 minutes. Lower the oven temperature to 350 degrees and bake 40 minutes more, until the top turns golden brown and the filling is bubbly and thickened. Remove the pie pan to a wire rack to cool before serving.

➤ Some Thoughts on Baking Pies ◀

If making pie crust intimidates you, there's only one way around it: Practice, practice, practice! When it comes to making pie crust and rolling it out, there's really no mastery involved. You'll learn over time when more water or flour is needed or if it's too hot to roll out a crust at noon! Confidence is key . . . and practice.

Here are a few points to remember when starting out:

Remove a chilled disk of dough from the refrigerator and let it stand on the counter for a few minutes to warm up before rolling. Why? Hard-chilled dough is difficult to roll, which means you work harder to do it, which means the dough shows that extra pressure in the end.

When rolling the dough, I always flour my rolling pin. Don't overflour the surface—the less you do to the dough, including handling it, the flakier it will be.

Always roll from the middle of the disk out to the edge in one direction, then give the disk a quarter turn and roll out again. Turning it helps keep the shape.

Roll the dough, don't press it out. You want to roll it out, not push it, into a round.

If the dough becomes sticky and soft while you're rolling it out, don't keep adding flour to the surface. Gather the dough into a ball and chill it until firm.

To transfer a round of dough to the pie pan, loop it gently over the rolling pin. Roll it a turn or two loosely, position the rolling pin over the pan, and unfurl the dough.

Press the dough gently into the pie pan. Should it tear, simply press it together again with your fingertips or use scraps of leftover dough to patch up any tears.

Most important of all, work the dough as little as possible. Overworking dough results in a dry, tough crust. If the dough keeps retracting when you're rolling it out, chances are it's already been overworked.

I love making pie crusts the old-fashioned way with the pastry cutter—they always turn out perfectly. But when rushed, I admit that the food processor really does the job.

Blueberry Cream Cheese Tart

➤ *Makes 10 to 12 servings* ◄

This beautiful, open-faced blueberry tart always gets rave reviews from my family and guests, and it's so simple to make!

Where I live in Utah, the blueberries are luscious and sweet, but the season is short. So I've suggested two toppings: one with fresh berries, the other with frozen, which makes this a true year-round fruit tart.

This is a good recipe for young bakers because so little stove work is involved. If your kids are helping, one word of caution: Buy about two to three times the amount of berries. They have a way of disappearing before they even make it to the topping. The tart won't last long, either.

➤ *Equipment Needed:* ★ 9-INCH TART PAN WITH STRAIGHT SIDES AND A RE-MOVABLE BOTTOM ★ ELECTRIC MIXER

❦ Crust:

1½ cups vanilla cookie crumbs

6 tablespoons (¾ stick) unsalted butter, melted

❦ Filling:

8 ounces cream cheese, softened

2 large eggs, at room temperature

½ cup sugar

1 tablespoon pure vanilla extract

2 teaspoons grated fresh lemon peel (see Tip: Grating Citrus Fruits, page 159)

2 cups fresh blueberries, picked over and rinsed; or frozen blueberries, thawed in a sieve set over a bowl to reserve the juice

2 tablespoons cornstarch

¼ teaspoon salt

¼ cup sugar

1 tablespoon fresh lemon juice

½ cup red currant jelly, melted and still warm

1 tablespoon cassis or raspberry liqueur (optional)

Whipped cream, as an accompaniment

1. Preheat the oven to 375 degrees F.

Make the crust:

2. In a bowl, combine the cookie crumbs and melted butter until thoroughly combined. Press the crust over the bottom and up the sides of the tart pan. Bake for 15 minutes. Remove the pan to a wire rack to cool.

Make the filling:

3. Put the cream cheese, eggs, sugar, vanilla, and lemon zest in a bowl and beat using an electric mixer on medium speed until well combined and smooth. Spoon the filling into the prebaked crust, spreading it evenly.

4. Bake for 20 to 30 minutes, or until the filling is firm. Remove the tart pan to a wire rack to cool.

5. While the filling is cooling, prepare the topping: If you are using thawed frozen blueberries, put the reserved liquid from the berries, cornstarch, salt, and remaining ¼ cup sugar

in a medium-size saucepan over medium heat. Cook, stirring, until thickened. Turn the heat to low and cook about 4 minutes more. Stir in the blueberries and lemon juice. Remove the pan from the heat and let the topping cool to lukewarm. Spoon the cooked topping over the tart, spreading it evenly, and then chill the tart for 2 hours.

6. If you are using fresh blueberries, toss the berries in the melted currant jelly in a bowl and stir in the cassis, if using. Arrange the glazed fresh berries over the filling.

7. To serve, remove the sides of the tart pan, place the tart on a serving plate, and serve it with a bowl of whipped cream.

Triangle Fruit Tart

➤ *Makes 12 servings* ➤

I call this my free-form pizza-wedge fruit tart! Instead of forming the pastry into the classic round, I form it into a triangle. And just as you do with pizza, you can finish this luscious tart the way you like best—simply, with just your favorite fruits, or as I have below, with pastry cream and fruit.

Both the shell and pastry cream can be prepared in advance, but for the best results assemble the tart just before serving. This tart is at its most delicious—creamy but light and refreshing—when all the textures remain intact.

A quick tip: If you don't have pie weights (small metal pebbles), you can use raw rice or dried beans as weights.

As for cutting this dramatic tart into equal pieces, it's difficult to be precise. A triangle is a tricky shape. I've found that what works best is if you first cut the tart into two smaller triangles, then cut the triangles into almost equal pieces. Anyone who gets a smaller piece as a first serving can always ask for more.

➤ *Equipment Needed:* ★ BAKING SHEET ★ PIE WEIGHTS

♥ Pastry:

2 cups all-purpose flour

3 tablespoons sugar

¹/₄ teaspoon salt

12 tablespoons (1¹/₂ sticks) cold unsalted
  butter, in pieces

2 large egg yolks, at room temperature

2 teaspoons pure vanilla extract

1 to 2 tablespoons ice water

♥ Pastry cream:

²/₃ cup sugar

¹/₂ cup all-purpose flour

Pinch of salt

2 cups light cream

6 large egg yolks, at room temperature

2 tablespoons unsalted butter

1 tablespoon pure vanilla extract

♥ Fruit topping:

1 cup red currant jelly

1 tablespoon fresh lemon juice

2 pints assorted fresh berries, such as
  raspberries, blueberries, and strawberries, hulled and halved, if necessary

4 to 6 kiwifruit, peeled and thinly sliced

Unsweetened whipped cream, as an
  accompaniment

Make the pastry:

1. Put the flour, sugar, and salt in a medium-size bowl and whisk together. With a pastry cutter, cut in the butter, a few pieces at a time, until the mixture is coarsely textured with
   small, irregular flakes and bits the size of small peas.

2. In a small bowl, stir together the egg yolks and vanilla. Add the yolk mixture to the dry ingredients and combine with a fork to moisten. Add the ice water, a tablespoon at a time,
   stirring to form a dough; then gather the dough with your hands and press it into a ball.
   Flatten the ball into the shape of a rough triangle, wrap it tightly in plastic wrap, and refrigerate it for 1 hour, or until firm.

3. On a floured surface, roll the pastry out to a ¹/₈-inch-thick triangle with approximately 14-
   inch equal sides. Transfer the pastry to a baking sheet and form sides, double-folding the
   dough. Press it with your fingers until about ³/₄ inch high. Flute the sides with your fingers.

Prick the dough all over with the tines of a fork, then put it on the baking sheet in the freezer, covered, for 15 minutes.

4. Preheat the oven to 425 degrees F.

5. Remove the chilled baking sheet from the freezer, line the inside of the triangle with foil, and cover the foil with pie weights. Bake the triangle on the middle rack for 18 minutes. Lower the oven temperature to 350 degrees F., remove the weights and foil, and bake 15 minutes more, or until the triangle is lightly golden brown. Remove the crust to a wire rack and let cool while preparing the pastry cream.

Make the pastry cream:

6. In a heavy, medium-size saucepan, whisk together the sugar, flour, and salt. Slowly stir in the light cream until smooth. Place the pan on the stove over medium-high heat and bring the mixture to a boil, stirring constantly. Lower the heat to maintain a simmer and cook, stirring, for 2 to 3 minutes.

7. In a bowl, lightly whisk together the egg yolks. Pour half of the hot cream mixture slowly over the yolks and whisk to combine. Pour the mixture back into the pan and cook over low heat, stirring constantly and being sure to stir the bottom and sides of the pan for about 5 minutes, until the mixture thickens and just starts to "steam." Do not let the mixture boil. It should heavily coat the back of the spoon.

8. Remove the pan from the heat. Stir in the butter and vanilla until smooth. Strain the pastry cream through a fine-mesh sieve into a bowl. Cover with plastic wrap directly on the surface, let cool to room temperature, then chill until cold, about 1 hour.

Make the fruit topping:

9. Place the tart shell on a decorative serving dish, fill it with the pastry cream, and smooth the surface.

10. In a small saucepan, heat the currant jelly until melted and stir in the lemon juice. Pour the glaze over the berries in a bowl and toss gently.

11. Arrange the berries and kiwi slices in a decorative pattern over the pastry cream. Cut the tart into triangles or squares and serve with unsweetened whipped cream as an accompaniment.

Berry Tartlets

*T*artlets are great for brunch or when you have more guests than places to seat them—they're the perfect finger food!

These are a breeze to put together. The shells can be prebaked at least one day in advance of serving. Wrap them with plastic wrap and store at room temperature. All you do after that is fill them and serve. Fill the shells as close to serving time as possible; that way the crusts remain crisp.

Over the summer, as more and more berries come into season, I love to vary the fruits. For a very pretty combination try a two-berry topping. These miniatures are great for little helping hands to garnish. My eight-year-old, Ashley, has an artistic touch—and calls these her edible art!

⇒ *Equipment Needed:* ★ SIX 4-INCH TART PANS WITH REMOVABLE BOTTOMS
★ PIE WEIGHTS

❦ Pastry:

2 cups all-purpose flour

2 tablespoons sugar

¼ teaspoon salt

12 tablespoons (1½ sticks) cold unsalted butter, cut into chunks

1 large egg yolk, at room temperature

1 teaspoon pure vanilla extract

2 to 3 tablespoons ice water

❦ White chocolate cream:

½ cup heavy cream

2 tablespoons unsalted butter

10 ounces white chocolate, chopped

1 cup currant jelly, heated and stirred until smooth

2 tablespoons crème de cassis
2 pints fresh raspberries

❦ Garnish:

Whipped cream

Make the pastry:

1. In a bowl, whisk together the flour, sugar, and salt. With a pastry cutter, cut in the butter until the mixture is coarsely textured with small, irregular flakes and bits the size of small peas. With a fork, stir in the egg yolk and vanilla. Stir in the water, 1 tablespoon at a time, until the dough just holds together. Gather the dough into a ball, flatten it into a disk, wrap it in plastic wrap, and chill for 1 hour.

Make the white chocolate cream:

2. In a medium-size ceramic or glass bowl covered with plastic wrap, heat the cream, butter, and chopped white chocolate on High in a microwave oven for 30-second intervals, stirring after each interval, until smooth. Set aside to cool slightly.

3. On a lightly floured surface, roll out the pastry dough to ⅛ inch thick. Using a tart pan as a guide, cut out 6 rounds. Press a round into each pan. With a fork, prick holes over the bottom of each crust and set in the freezer for 20 minutes.

4. Preheat the oven to 400 degrees F.

5. Line each tart pan with aluminum foil, cover with pie weights, and bake on a baking sheet for 15 minutes. Lower the oven temperature to 350 degrees F., remove the weights and foil, and bake 15 minutes more. Remove from the baking sheet and cool on wire racks.

Assemble the tartlets:

6. In a bowl, gently fold the warm currant jelly and crème de cassis over the berries in a bowl.

7. Remove the pastry shells from the tart pans. Divide the white chocolate cream evenly among the cooled tart shells and arrange the fresh berries on top. Chill for 1 hour.

8. Serve the tartlets garnished with dollops of whipped cream.

Puff Pastry Pear Tart

> ⇒ *Serves 12 to 14* ⇐

*P*uff pastry has been adopted by American bakers as if it were their own! This exquisitely flaky, many-layered butter-rich pastry is French in origin and requires a baker's touch (or a lot of practice) to be made well. Luckily, good puff pastry dough is commercially made and is available in the freezer section of most supermarkets; it is sometimes sold by fine bakeries as well. Buy a box and keep it in your freezer; then when you want to make this simple tart, you'll be all set.

This elegant fruit strip combines pears, almonds, and pastry but it's flexible. Use what fruit you have on hand.

⇒ *Equipment Needed:* ★ 4 BY 14-INCH TART PAN ★ ELECTRIC MIXER

2 sheets frozen puff pastry, thawed according to the package directions

❦ Filling:

8 ounces cream cheese, softened

½ cup sugar

1 large egg, at room temperature

1 teaspoon pure vanilla extract

¾ cup sliced almonds, toasted

3 ripe pears, peeled, cored, and thinly sliced

❦ Glaze:

1 cup apricot jelly

1 teaspoon pure almond extract

Cinnamon, for dusting (optional)

Make the filling:

1. Put the cream cheese and sugar in a large bowl and beat until smooth using the electric mixer on medium speed. Beat in the egg and vanilla until combined. Scrape down the bowl. On low speed, beat the mixture until smooth. Set the filling aside.
2. Preheat the oven to 375 degrees F.

3. In a small saucepan over low heat, warm the jelly, stirring until melted and smooth. Remove the pan from the heat and stir in the almond extract.

Prepare the pastry:

4. On a lightly floured surface, roll out 1 sheet of the puff pastry into a 5 by 15-inch rectangle. Carefully fit it over the bottom and up the sides of the tart pan, leaving a ¼-inch overhang; trim off any excess dough. Prick the bottom and sides of the dough with a fork.

Assemble the tart:

5. Pour the cream cheese filling into the dough-lined tart pan and smooth the surface. Sprinkle the almonds over the filling, then carefully layer the pear slices in diagonal rows over the filling.

6. Brush the pears with the apricot glaze.

7. On a lightly floured surface, roll out the remaining sheet of puff pastry into a 5 by 15-inch rectangle. Dust lightly with flour, then fold in half lengthwise. With a small, sharp knife, cut 8 to 10 evenly spaced ½-inch-wide slits along the folded edge of the pastry.

8. Brush the top edges of the pastry in the pan lightly with water. Place the cut sheet of pastry over the pan and carefully unfold it to fit over the top of the tart pan. Trim the pastry if necessary, then crimp the edges to seal. If desired, sprinkle the top of the tart with cinnamon.

9. Bake for 35 to 40 minutes, until the crust is golden brown. Remove from the oven to a wire rack and cool slightly before serving.

Cherry Pie

➤ *Makes 12 servings* ◄

*T*here is something about a lattice-topped cherry pie, simply presented and beautifully baked, that says America to me. I love it almost as much as I do apple pie! So here's my version, in all its old-fashioned splendor—it's not too sweet, and the best I've ever tasted.

Once upon a time, cherry pie was made with fresh cherries. Cherries are a delicate fruit, and much of the crop in the United States, the largest producer, is reserved for canning and preserving. Don't confuse tart red cherries, used here, with the sweet dark cherries packed in syrup. They're not the same and can't be substituted for each other. Also, use the amount of sugar we have called for in the filling. It may seem a lot, but tart cherries are just that, *very* tart, and also very delicious!

➤ *Equipment Needed:* ★ 9-INCH DEEP-DISH PIE PAN

❦ Crust:

2¹/₂ cups all-purpose flour

¹/₄ teaspoon salt

16 tablespoons (2 sticks) cold unsalted butter,
    cut into chunks

6 to 7 tablespoons ice water

❦ Filling:

1¹/₂ cups sugar

5 tablespoons cornstarch

Two 16-ounce cans tart, pitted red
    cherries, drained; reserve 1 cup of the juice

2 tablespoons maraschino cherry juice

2 tablespoons unsalted butter

❦ Eggwash:

1 egg, lightly beaten

2 teaspoons sugar

Make the crust:

1. In a bowl, whisk together the flour and salt. With a pastry cutter, cut in the butter until the mixture is coarsely textured with small, irregular flakes and bits the size of small peas. Sprinkle on the water, 1 tablespoon at a time, stirring with a fork until the dough just holds together. Gather the dough into 2 balls, one slightly larger than the other, flatten into disks, wrap each separately in plastic wrap, and chill for 1 hour.

Make the filling:

2. In a large, heavy-bottomed saucepan, whisk together the sugar and cornstarch. Over medium-high heat, slowly whisk in the reserved cherry juice until smooth, and bring to a boil, stirring constantly until thickened. Gently stir in the cherries and maraschino juice, and bring the mixture back to a boil. Remove from the heat and stir in the butter. Transfer to a bowl set on a wire rack to cool slightly while preparing the crust.

3. Preheat the oven to 425 degrees F.

Assemble the pie:

4. On a lightly floured surface, roll out the larger disk of dough into a ⅛-inch-thick round at least 2 inches larger in diameter than the pie pan. Transfer the dough to the pan and trim the edges to a 1-inch overhang. Chill the pan in the freezer while rolling out the top.

5. Roll out the remaining dough piece into a ⅛-inch-thick round. Cut it into 12 strips, each ¾ inch wide.

6. Remove the pan from the freezer and pour in the filling. Top with the dough strips in a latticework pattern. Fold the edges of the bottom crust over the ends of the strips and then crimp with your fingers to seal.

7. Brush the lattice strips with the eggwash. Sprinkle the strips with sugar.

8. Bake on the middle rack of the oven for 20 minutes. Lower the oven temperature to 350 degrees F. and bake 30 to 40 minutes more, until the lattice strips are golden brown and the filling is bubbly. Transfer the pie to a wire rack to cool for 1 hour before serving.

Triple Cherry Chocolate Pie

*H*ow do you improve on a classic tart cherry pie? Try this open-faced chocolate pie with three kinds of cherries and a crumb topping! You won't believe how beautifully chocolate and cherries go together. The combination of colors and textures alone is incredible. Look for dried cherries in health-food stores and supermarkets.

➤ *Equipment Needed:* ★ 9-INCH DEEP-DISH PIE PAN

❧ Crust:

1½ cups all-purpose flour

¼ cup unsweetened cocoa powder

2 tablespoons sugar

8 tablespoons (1 stick) cold unsalted butter, cut into chunks

4 to 5 tablespoons ice water

❧ Filling:

1 cup sugar

6 tablespoons cornstarch

24 ounces frozen dark, sweet, pitted cherries, thawed and drained; reserve the juice

One 14½-ounce can tart, pitted red cherries, drained; reserve the juice

1 cup dried cherries

❧ Topping:

¼ cup all-purpose flour

2 tablespoons quick oats (not *instant*)

2 tablespoons light brown sugar

2 tablespoons unsalted butter, melted

2 ounces semisweet chocolate, chopped

Make the crust:

1. In a bowl, whisk together the flour, cocoa, and sugar. With a pastry cutter, cut in the butter until the mixture is coarsely textured with small, irregular flakes and bits the size of

small peas. Sprinkle on the water, 1 tablespoon at a time, stirring with a fork until the dough just holds together. Gather the dough into a ball, flatten into a disk, wrap in plastic, and chill for 1 hour.

Make the filling:

2. In a heavy-bottomed saucepan, whisk together the sugar and cornstarch.
3. Combine both of the reserved cherry juices to equal 1 cup; discard any remaining juice. Stir the juice into the sugar mixture until smooth. Over medium-high heat, bring the sauce to a boil, stirring constantly. Lower the heat and cook until thickened.
4. Gently stir in all the cherries and bring the mixture back to a boil. Remove the pan from the heat and transfer the filling to a bowl to cool slightly while preparing the crust.
5. Preheat the oven to 375 degrees F.
6. On a lightly floured surface, roll out the dough into a ⅛-inch-thick round. Fit into the pie pan, trim the edges if necessary, and crimp decoratively. Chill while preparing the topping.

Make the topping:

7. In a small bowl, whisk together the flour, oats, and sugar. Stir in the melted butter and combine thoroughly.

Assemble the pie:

8. Pour the filling into the chilled crust. Sprinkle the chopped chocolate over the filling. Crumble the topping over all.
9. Bake on the middle rack of the oven for 50 to 55 minutes, until the filling is bubbly and the topping turns golden brown.
10. Transfer the pie pan to a wire rack and cool before serving.

Chapter 3

Cheesecakes

Did you know that cheesecake can be traced back nearly three thousand years? The Greeks enjoyed a form of it and even fed it to their athletes before they competed in the Olympic Games. It wasn't until the fifteenth century, though, that cheesecake became, and remained, popular in Europe. It was brought to these shores, like so many other good things, by immigrants who came to settle here.

There are two distinct types of cheesecake in the United States: New York style, which uses cream cheese in the filling; and Italian style, which uses ricotta cheese. As you'll see from this chapter, I'm a New York–style cheesecake fan through and through and prefer to use a crumb crust. I just love the contrast between the smoothness of the filling and the crunchy, crumbly texture on the outside.

How you bake cheesecake is crucial to its taste and texture. It must be done slowly, with low heat and lots of moisture. Even with slow heat, the top of your cheesecake may crack. Not to worry. Your cake will taste every bit as good. And please don't try to hurry the cooling of a cheesecake, either. I always suggest making it the day before you plan to serve it.

I've included cheesecakes for every taste. There are cheesecakes for both dark and white chocolate lovers, as well as two very unique seasonal cheesecakes that call for a pureed vegetable filling, either of which would be perfect for Thanksgiving. The last two recipes in the chapter are among the ones I like best: One features butterscotch and the other tart citrus flavors.

I admit that cheesecake is a wickedly rich dessert, but treat yourself to one of these very special creations—you deserve it!

Debbi's New York—Style Cheesecake

➤ *Makes 12 servings* ◄

*N*ew York–style cheesecakes are renowned for their incredible creaminess. The texture comes from the use of extravagant amounts of cream cheese, often combined with sour cream. New York–style cheesecake can be plain or fancy, with crust or without, topped or not. They are not to be confused with Italian-style cheesecakes that use ricotta cheese and have a fluffier texture.

I love New York–style cheesecake with strawberry topping, but this version always gets raves. I've used a crumb crust of spicy gingersnaps and sweetened it a little with toffee bits. Melted toffee bits crown the top. It's crunchy, it's creamy, it's unique—it's great!

Long, slow baking ensures the right texture for cheesecakes in general. I've had to encourage my daughters to resist the temptation to open the oven door for at least the first half hour. A draft or even a little jarring can cause the cake to fall. And don't ever rush the baking or cooling of a cheesecake. (My husband, Randy, has never been that patient. After years of warnings, I still find his fork marks on the cheesecake!) I always bake my cheesecakes a day ahead of when I plan to serve them, because, like spaghetti sauce, the flavor of a cheesecake improves—it's always better the next day.

It may seem obvious, but don't try to make cheesecake with anything but real cream cheese. Reduced-fat varieties just won't do!

➤ *Equipment Needed:* ★ 9-INCH SPRINGFORM PAN ★ ELECTRIC MIXER

❦ Crust:

½ cup butter toffee bits

2 cups gingersnap cookie crumbs

4 tablespoons (½ stick) unsalted butter, melted

❦ Filling:

16 ounces cream cheese, softened

1 cup sugar

3 large eggs, at room temperature

1½ cups sour cream

1 tablespoon pure vanilla extract

½ cup butter toffee bits

½ cup caramel sauce, jarred or homemade (page 97), warmed

1. Preheat the oven to 300 degrees F. Butter the springform pan.

Make the crust:

2. In a large bowl, combine the toffee bits with the crumbs and stir in the butter until thoroughly combined. Press the crust over the bottom and up the sides of the prepared pan, then chill the pan in the refrigerator while preparing the filling.

Make the filling:

3. Put the cream cheese and sugar in a large bowl and beat until smooth using the electric mixer on medium speed. Add the eggs, 1 at a time, beating for 20 seconds after each addition. Add the sour cream and vanilla, and beat until smooth. Scrape down the bowl. Pour the filling into the prepared crust and smooth the top.

4. Fill a 2-quart baking pan halfway with hot water and place on the bottom rack of the oven. Bake the cake on the middle rack for 1¼ hours. Turn off the oven and leave the cake in for 30 minutes with the door closed. Remove the cake to a wire rack and cool to room temperature, about 1 hour. Cover the cake with foil and refrigerate for 4 hours or overnight.

Make the topping:

5. Before serving, stir the toffee bits into the warm caramel sauce. Pour over the top of the cheesecake.

6. To serve, transfer the cake to a serving plate and remove the sides of the springform pan. Slice the cake with a sharp, thin knife, wiping the blade clean after each cut.

Chocolate Espresso Cheesecake

➤ *Makes 12 servings* ◄

What do you think happens if you add melted chocolate and a little strong coffee to the cream cheese and sour cream that give New York–style cheesecake its incredible delicious creaminess? Incredibly delicious chocolate creaminess—that's what happens!

I admit that this cheesecake is extravagant, with melted chocolate drizzled over the crust and chocolate cream crowning the filling. But this is a "wow," according to our recent dinner guests, who oohed and aahed about this dessert. And while I was busy entertaining them, Ashley and McKenzie ate mine!

If you're planning to serve this to a big group, serve it as I do: alongside New York–style cheesecake. Pairing them makes for the most sensational contrast.

➤ *Equipment Needed:* ★ 9-INCH SPRINGFORM PAN ★ ELECTRIC MIXER

❦ Crust:

1 1/2 cups ground pecans, toasted

1 1/2 cups chocolate wafer cookie crumbs

6 tablespoons (3/4 stick) unsalted butter, melted

3 ounces semisweet chocolate, melted

❦ Filling:

16 ounces cream cheese, softened

1 cup firmly packed dark brown sugar

4 large eggs, at room temperature

2 teaspoons pure vanilla extract

8 ounces semisweet chocolate, melted (see How
to Melt Chocolate, page 18)

1/3 cup fresh-brewed espresso or other strong coffee

1 cup sour cream

❦ Glaze:

1/3 cup heavy cream

1 tablespoon sugar

3 ounces semisweet chocolate, chopped

1. Preheat the oven to 300 degrees F. Lightly butter the springform pan.

Make the crust:

2. In a bowl, combine the pecans and cookie crumbs, and stir in the butter until combined. Press the crust over the bottom and up the sides of the prepared pan. Drizzle the crust with the melted chocolate. Chill the crust while preparing the filling.

Make the filling:

3. Put the cream cheese and brown sugar in a bowl and beat until smooth using the electric mixer on medium speed. Scrape down the bowl. Add the eggs, 1 at a time, beating for 20 seconds after each addition. Add the vanilla and melted chocolate and beat on low speed until combined. Pour in the espresso and beat until combined. Add the sour cream and beat until smooth and fully combined. Scrape down the bowl. Pour the filling into the prepared crust and smooth the top.

4. Fill a 2-quart pan halfway with hot water and place on the bottom rack of the oven. Bake the cake on the middle rack for 1 hour. Lower the oven temperature to 275 degrees F. and bake the cake 1 hour more. Lower the oven temperature to 250 degrees F. and bake 30 minutes more. Turn off the oven and leave the cake in for 30 minutes more with the door

closed. Remove the cake to a wire rack and cool to room temperature. Cover the cake with foil and refrigerate for at least 4 hours or overnight.

Make the glaze:

5. In a ceramic or glass bowl covered with plastic wrap, heat the cream, sugar, and chocolate on High in a microwave oven for 30-second intervals, stirring after each interval, until smooth.
6. Pour the warm glaze over the top of the cheesecake and spread until smooth. Chill the cake for 1 hour to set the glaze.
7. To serve, transfer the cake to a serving plate and remove the sides of the springform pan. Slice the cake with a sharp, thin knife, wiping the blade clean after each cut.

Pumpkin Cheesecake

➤ Makes 12 servings ◄

I dedicate this cheesecake to Randy, who finally gave me my wedding ring, which said "From Denver (where we met) to Eternity." I've made him many pumpkin recipes since then because he loves pumpkin anything. When I was pregnant with our first daughter, Jessica, *he* had a craving for pumpkin ice cream. After searching all night for an ice cream parlor, we found it, and ever since, anything pumpkin is a hit at the Fields' family home, anytime!

Like all cheesecake, bake this with slow heat and lots of patience. You'll be tying up your oven for three hours for the baking of this cake alone. Luckily, cheesecakes are best made one day in advance of serving. Think of it this way: You'll have less to do on the holiday!

➤ *Equipment Needed:* ★ 9-INCH SPRINGFORM PAN ★ ELECTRIC MIXER

❦ Crust:

2 cups finely ground, toasted pecans

1 cup chopped pecans, toasted

⅔ cup vanilla wafer crumbs

⅓ cup graham cracker crumbs

3 tablespoons unsalted butter, melted

❦ Filling:

8 ounces cream cheese, softened

2 tablespoons unsalted butter, softened

½ cup firmly packed dark brown sugar

¼ cup white sugar

3 large eggs, at room temperature

One 15-ounce can pumpkin puree (not *pie filling*)

½ cup sour cream

3 tablespoons all-purpose flour

1½ teaspoons pumpkin pie spice

2 teaspoons pure vanilla extract

1. Preheat the oven to 300 degrees F. Lightly butter the springform pan.

Make the crust:

2. In a bowl, combine the ground pecans, chopped pecans, vanilla wafer crumbs, and graham cracker crumbs with the butter and stir until combined. Press the crust over the bottom and up the sides of the springform pan. Bake for 15 minutes, then set the pan aside.

Make the filling:

3. Put the cream cheese, butter, brown and white sugars in a bowl and beat until smooth using the electric mixer on medium speed. Scrape down the bowl. Add the eggs, 1 at a time, beating for 20 seconds after each addition. Add the pumpkin puree and sour cream, and beat until smooth. Add the flour, pie spice, and vanilla, beating to combine well. Scrape down the bowl. Pour the filling into the prebaked crust and smooth the top.

4. Fill a 2-quart baking pan halfway with hot water and place on the bottom rack of the oven. Bake the cake on the middle rack for 1 hour. Lower the oven temperature to 275 degrees F. and bake 1 hour more. Turn the oven off and leave the cake in with the door closed for 1 hour more. Remove the cake to a wire rack and let cool completely. Cover the cake with foil and refrigerate at least 4 hours or overnight.

5. To serve, transfer the cake to a serving plate and remove the sides of the springform pan. Slice the cake with a sharp, thin knife, wiping the blade clean after each cut.

Sweet Potato—Pecan Cheesecake
with Chocolate Crust

> ➤ *Makes 12 servings* ◄

*S*weet potato cheesecake is a favorite of mine that captures the pleasures of southern sweet potato pie but in a more luxurious, creamy way. Every Thanksgiving we adopt any family or friends who might be alone for the holiday, and I usually whip up five or six desserts. This is a family favorite, and a great way to get the kids to taste a new vegetable, since it's sweet and they can help make it.

Mash your own sweet potatoes if you want to, or use canned yams as a substitute. Just be sure that neither is sweetened or candied in any way.

➤ *Equipment Needed:* ★ 9-INCH SPRINGFORM PAN ★ ELECTRIC MIXER

❦ Crust:

1½ cups finely chopped, toasted pecans

1½ cups finely crushed chocolate wafer crumbs

4 tablespoons sugar

4 tablespoons (½ stick) unsalted butter, melted

❦ Filling:

16 ounces cream cheese, softened

15 ounces whole-milk ricotta

1 cup firmly packed light brown sugar

½ cup white sugar

5 large eggs, at room temperature

One 15-ounce can sweet potatoes or yams, drained and mashed until smooth

2 tablespoons all-purpose flour

1 tablespoon pumpkin pie spice

1 tablespoon brandy

2 teaspoons pure vanilla extract

❦ Garnish:

3 ounces semisweet chocolate, melted

12 pecan halves, toasted

1. Preheat the oven to 300 degrees F. Lightly butter the springform pan.

Make the crust:

2. In a medium bowl, combine the pecans, wafer crumbs, and sugar, and stir in the butter until combined. Press the crust over the bottom and up the sides of the prepared pan. Chill the pan while preparing the filling.

Make the filling:

3. Put the cream cheese and ricotta in a large bowl and beat until smooth and creamy using the electric mixer on medium speed. Add the brown and white sugars and beat until smooth. Scrape down the bowl. Add the eggs, 1 at a time, beating for 20 seconds after each addition. Add the mashed sweet potato, flour, pie spice, brandy, and vanilla, and beat until smooth. Scrape down the bowl. Pour the filling into the prepared crust and smooth the top.

4. Fill a 2-quart baking pan halfway with hot water and place on the bottom rack of the oven. Bake the cake on the middle rack for 1 hour. Lower the oven temperature to 275 degrees F. and bake 1 hour more. Turn off the oven and leave the cake in with the door closed for 30 minutes. Remove the cake to a wire rack and cool to room temperature. Cover the cake with foil and refrigerate for at least 4 hours or overnight.

Garnish the cake:

5. Pour the melted chocolate over the top of the cheesecake and set the pecan halves evenly spaced around the edge.

6. To serve, transfer the cake to a serving plate and remove the sides of the springform pan. Slice the cake with a sharp, thin knife, wiping the blade clean after each cut.

Chocolate Raspberry Cheesecake

➤ *Makes 12 servings* ◄

The flavors of chocolate and raspberry were meant for each other, so it seemed only natural to combine them in one luscious dessert. This cake is as pretty to look at as it is good to eat, and it is intense with raspberry flavor. The raspberry flavor here comes from raspberry liqueur, also known as *framboise,* and is further heightened by a garnish of raspberry puree and fresh berries.

I always want you to take care melting chocolate. No matter which method you choose, the chocolate should be absolutely smooth when you're done. For pointers see How to Melt Chocolate, page 18.

➤ *Equipment Needed:* ★ 9-INCH SPRINGFORM PAN ★ ELECTRIC MIXER
★ FOOD PROCESSOR WITH METAL BLADE

❦ Crust:

1 cup chocolate wafer crumbs

2 tablespoons sugar

2 tablespoons all-purpose flour

4 tablespoons (½ stick) unsalted butter, melted

❦ Filling:

24 ounces cream cheese, softened

½ cup sugar

4 large eggs, at room temperature

8 ounces semisweet chocolate, melted

¼ cup raspberry liqueur

½ cup heavy cream

1 tablespoon pure vanilla extract

❦ Topping:

1 cup sour cream

⅓ cup firmly packed light brown sugar

❦ Sauce:

12 ounces frozen sweetened raspberries, thawed

¼ cup sugar

1 tablespoon raspberry liqueur

2 pints fresh raspberries (optional)

1. Preheat the oven to 300 degrees F. Lightly butter the springform pan.

Make the crust:

2. In a bowl, combine the chocolate wafer crumbs, sugar, and flour, and stir in the butter until combined. Press the crust over the bottom and up the sides of the prepared pan. Bake for 15 minutes. Set the pan aside to cool.

Make the filling:

3. Put the cream cheese and sugar in a large bowl and beat until smooth using the electric mixer on medium speed. Scrape down the bowl. Add the eggs, 1 at a time, beating for 20

seconds after each addition. Scrape down the bowl. Add the melted chocolate, raspberry liqueur, cream, and vanilla, and beat until smooth. Scrape down the bowl. Pour the filling into the prepared crust and smooth the top.

4. Fill a 2-quart baking pan halfway with hot water and place on the bottom rack of the oven. Bake the cake on the middle rack for 1 hour. Lower the oven temperature to 275 degrees F. and bake 1 hour more. Turn off the oven and leave the cake in for 30 minutes with the door closed. Remove the cake to a wire rack and cool to room temperature.

Make the topping:

5. In a bowl, combine the sour cream and sugar until smooth. Pour over the top of the cake and spread until smooth. Cover the cake with foil and chill for at least 4 hours or overnight.

Make the sauce:

6. Combine all the sauce ingredients and puree until smooth in the food processor. Strain the puree through a fine-mesh sieve into a bowl, cover, and chill until cold.

7. To serve, top the cake with fresh raspberries, if desired, and pour half of the sauce over them. Serve the remaining sauce separately. Or ladle a pool of the sauce onto each dessert plate and arrange a slice of the cheesecake on it.

White Chocolate Chunk Cheesecake

Makes 12 servings

*T*his white chocolate cheesecake is a one-of-a-kind special dessert. I assure you that the extra attention this recipe needs pays off in the end when you serve it.

Please buy the very best white chocolate available. Not all white chocolate is the same. The best-quality white chocolate must contain cocoa butter. Read the label, and keep looking until you find the one that does. Then buy almost 2 pounds of it, which is what you need for this cake!

I've suggested that you melt the white chocolate over barely simmering water. Pay attention, because white chocolate has a tendency to scorch and seize up more easily than dark chocolate does. Should that happen and the chocolate becomes grainy, add a drop or two of vegetable oil to it and stir until smooth.

➤ *Equipment Needed:* ★ 9-INCH SPRINGFORM PAN ★ ELECTRIC MIXER

❦ Crust:

1 cup graham cracker crumbs

2 tablespoons all-purpose flour

2 tablespoons sugar

4 tablespoons (½ stick) unsalted butter, melted

❦ Filling:

1¼ pounds premium white chocolate, cut into small pieces; reserve ¼ pound

3 large egg whites, at room temperature

Pinch of cream of tartar

3 tablespoons sugar

12 ounces cream cheese, softened

1 cup sour cream

1 tablespoon pure vanilla extract

2 large egg yolks, at room temperature

❦ Garnish

8 ounces premium white chocolate, cut into small pieces

¼ cup heavy cream

1. Preheat the oven to 325 degrees F. Lightly butter the springform pan.

Make the crust:

2. In a bowl, combine the graham cracker crumbs, flour, and sugar, and stir in the butter until combined. Press the crust over the bottom and one-quarter of the way up the sides of the prepared pan. Bake for 15 minutes. Set the pan aside to cool.

Make the filling:

3. In the top of a double boiler set over barely simmering water, melt 1 pound of the chopped white chocolate, stirring occasionally until smooth. Remove the pan from the heat and cool.

4. Put the egg whites in a bowl and beat until frothy using the electric mixer on medium speed. Add the cream of tartar and beat until soft peaks form. Slowly add the sugar and beat until stiff peaks form. Set aside.

5. Put the cream cheese in a large bowl and beat until smooth using the electric mixer on medium speed. Add the sour cream and vanilla. Add the egg yolks, 1 at a time, beating for 20 seconds after each addition. Beat in the melted white chocolate on low speed until combined.

6. Fold one-third of the beaten whites into the batter to lighten it, then fold in the remaining whites gently but thoroughly. Fold in the reserved ¼ pound chopped white chocolate and combine well. Scrape down the bowl. Pour the filling into the prepared crust and smooth the top.

7. Fill a 2-quart baking pan halfway with hot water and place on the bottom rack of the oven. Bake the cake on the middle rack for 1 hour. Turn off the oven and leave the cake in for 2 hours with the door closed. Cover the cake with foil and refrigerate for at least 4 hours or overnight.

Make the garnish:

8. In a ceramic or glass bowl covered with plastic wrap, heat the chocolate with the cream on High in a microwave oven for 30-second intervals, stirring after each interval, until smooth.

9. Pour the warm glaze over the chilled cheesecake and spread it until smooth. Chill for 1 hour to set glaze.

10. To serve, transfer the cake to a serving plate and remove the sides of the springform pan. Slice the cake with a sharp, thin knife, wiping the blade clean after each cut.

Butterscotch Cheesecake

I love both the flavor and the color of butterscotch and have always wanted to combine it with cream cheese and sour cream in a cheesecake dessert. This incredible cheesecake does the trick!

The graham cracker crust and the filling are a breeze to make. Storebought caramel sauce can even be used for the topping. If you've the time to make your own caramel, do so by all means. Just don't run out of time and forgo the topping. The bits of turtle candy in caramel sauce put this cheesecake . . . well, right over the top!

Equipment Needed: ★ 9-INCH SPRINGFORM PAN ★ ELECTRIC MIXER

❦ Crust:

1 cup graham cracker crumbs	*2 tablespoons sugar*
2 tablespoons flour	*4 tablespoons (½ stick) unsalted butter, melted*

❦ Filling:

12 ounces butterscotch chips	*4 large eggs, at room temperature*
¼ cup heavy cream	*1 cup sour cream*
16 ounces cream cheese, softened	*2 tablespoons flour*
½ cup firmly packed light brown sugar	*1 tablespoon pure vanilla extract*

❦ Garnish:

One 8-ounce jar caramel topping, warmed	*One 8-ounce package Turtle candies, chopped*

1. Preheat the oven to 325 degrees F. Lightly butter the springform pan.

Make the crust:

2. In a bowl, combine the graham cracker crumbs, flour, and sugar, and stir in the butter until thoroughly blended. Press the crust over the bottom and one-quarter of the way up the sides of the prepared pan. Bake for 15 minutes, then set the pan aside to cool.

Make the filling:

3. In the top of a double boiler set over barely simmering water, melt the butterscotch chips with the heavy cream, stirring until smooth and creamy. Remove the pan from the heat.

4. Put the cream cheese and brown sugar in a large bowl and beat until smooth using the electric mixer on medium speed. Add the eggs, 1 at a time, beating for 20 seconds after each addition. Scrape down the bowl. Add the sour cream, flour, and vanilla, and beat until smooth. Add the butterscotch mixture and beat on low speed until smooth. Scrape down the bowl. Pour the filling into the prepared pan and smooth the top.

5. Fill a 2-quart baking pan halfway with hot water and place on the bottom rack of the oven. Bake the cake on the middle rack for 1 hour. Turn off the oven and leave the cake in for 1 hour with the door closed. Remove the cake to a wire rack and cool to room temperature. Cover the cake with foil and refrigerate for at least 4 hours or overnight.

6. Drizzle half of the warm caramel sauce over the cake. Sprinkle the chopped Turtle candies evenly over the caramel. Drizzle the remaining caramel over the candies.

7. To serve, transfer the cake to a serving plate and remove the sides of the springform pan. Slice the cake with a sharp, thin knife, wiping the blade clean after each cut.

Creamy Citrus Cheesecake

➤ *Makes 12 servings* ◄

*L*ight and refreshing are the first two words that come immediately to mind when describing this cheesecake. The reason? It's topped with the most marvelous lemony orange curd that flavors the cake from the top down and melds with the fresh lime juice and peel in the silky cream cheese and sour cream batter.

Serve this slightly chilled on a warm summer's day or try it during the winter when you're just longing for the first hint of spring. If you prefer a sweeter garnish than fresh lime, halved orange slices make a very pretty presentation, too. Prettier still would be beautiful blood oranges with their dramatic red-orange color. It's another great way to take advantage of their seasonal availability.

➤ *Equipment Needed:* ★ 9-INCH SPRINGFORM PAN ★ ELECTRIC MIXER

❦ Crust:

1¼ cups graham cracker crumbs

4 tablespoons (½ stick) unsalted butter, melted

1½ teaspoons grated fresh lime peel (see Tip: Grating Citrus Fruits, page 159)

❦ Filling:

24 ounces cream cheese, softened

1 cup sugar

3 large eggs, at room temperature

8 ounces sour cream

¼ cup fresh lime juice

½ teaspoon pure vanilla extract

½ teaspoon pure almond extract

1 tablespoon grated fresh lime peel

❦ Lemon-orange curd:

4 large egg yolks, at room temperature, beaten

¾ cup sugar

2 tablespoons fresh lemon juice

2 tablespoons fresh orange juice

4 tablespoons (½ stick) cold unsalted butter, cut into chunks

❦ Garnish:

Thin half-moon slices of lime
Slivers of orange peel

1. Preheat the oven to 325 degrees F. Lightly butter the springform pan.

Make the crust:

2. In a bowl, combine the graham cracker crumbs, butter, and peel. Press the crust over the bottom and halfway up the sides of the pan. Chill the pan while making the filling.

Make the filling:

3. Put the cream cheese and sugar in a large bowl and beat until smooth, using the electric mixer at medium speed. Scrape down the bowl. Add the eggs, 1 at a time, beating for 20 seconds after each addition. Scrape down the bowl. Add the sour cream and beat until smooth. Add the lime juice, vanilla, and almond extracts, and peel, and beat until combined. Scrape down the bowl. Pour the filling into the prepared crust and smooth the top.

4. Fill a 2-quart baking pan halfway with hot water and place on the bottom rack of the oven. Bake the cake on the middle rack for 1 hour. Turn off the oven and leave the cake in for 1 hour with the door closed. Remove the cake to a wire rack and cool to room temperature.

Make the lemon-orange curd:

5. In the top of a double boiler set over barely simmering water, whisk together the egg yolks and sugar until combined. Slowly stir in the lemon and orange juices until smooth. Cook the mixture, stirring constantly with a wooden spoon, until thickened, 10 to 15 minutes. It should heavily coat the back of the spoon. Remove the pan from the heat and stir in the butter until smooth. Strain the hot curd through a fine-mesh sieve into a bowl and let cool slightly.

Assemble the cake:

6. Pour the curd over the cheesecake, then refrigerate the cake, covered with foil, for at least 4 hours or overnight.

7. To serve, transfer the cake to a serving plate, garnish it with the lime slices and orange slivers, and remove the sides of the springform pan. Slice the cake with a sharp, thin knife, wiping the blade clean after each cut.

Chapter 4

Cream, Nut, and Meringue Pies

W HEN I FOUND I had to select only a handful of recipes from the great tradition of pie making in America, I immediately turned to my personal favorites. And even then it wasn't easy. There are so many different kinds of wonderful American pies.

Eventually I narrowed it down to cream pies, nut pies, and meringue pies because each offers something different and holds a special place in people's hearts.

Cream pies can be dressed up or down depending on how much cream you want to add for garnish. See my Chocolate Cream Pie on page 99.

No collection on American pies could ever be considered complete without that great contribution from the South: pecan pie, one of my family's favorites, and so easy to make. My favorite pecan pie, on page 92, isn't too sweet, but it uses my special touch, a lot of extra nuts for added crunch. And because I love pecans and chocolate, I couldn't resist the urge to combine them in an extravagant pie.

Last but not least are the meringue pies—chocolate, lemon, and Key lime. In my mind, these layered pies are quintessentially American and they are truly irresistible.

Coconut Cream Pie

*F*or me, coconut cream pie is pure comfort food. What could be better than a flaky home-made crust filled with smooth custard that's flecked with sweetened coconut? I've added some whipped cream for a topping and a few macadamia nuts for crunch. Take a bite of this, close your eyes, and imagine you're on a beach in Hawaii. That's how tropical the flavors are!

For best results, prebake the crust and make the custard in advance, but assemble the pie with just enough time for it to chill. You want the crust crisp, not soggy.

≥ *Equipment Needed:* ★ 9-INCH DEEP-DISH PIE PAN ★ PIE WEIGHTS
  ★ ELECTRIC MIXER

❦ Crust:

1½ cups all-purpose flour

2 tablespoons sugar

¼ teaspoon salt

8 tablespoons (1 stick) cold unsalted butter, cut into chunks

3 to 4 tablespoons ice water

❦ Coconut custard:

⅔ cup sugar

¼ cup cornstarch

Pinch of salt

2 cups half-and-half

6 large egg yolks, at room temperature, lightly beaten

2 tablespoons unsalted butter

1 tablespoon pure vanilla extract

1¼ cups shredded sweetened coconut, lightly toasted (see Tip: Toasting Coconut, page 21)

❦ Whipped Cream:

1 cup heavy cream, chilled

1 tablespoon powdered sugar

1 teaspoon pure vanilla extract

❦ Garnish:

¼ cup shredded sweetened coconut, lightly toasted

¼ cup chopped macadamia nuts, toasted

Make the crust:

1. In a bowl, whisk together the flour, sugar, and salt. With a pastry cutter, cut in the butter until the mixture is coarsely textured with small, irregular flakes and bits the size of small peas. Sprinkle on the water, 1 tablespoon at a time, stirring with a fork until the dough just holds together. Gather the dough into a ball, flatten it into a disk, wrap it in plastic wrap, and chill for 1 hour.

Make the custard:

2. In a heavy-bottomed saucepan, whisk together the sugar, cornstarch, and salt. Slowly stir in the half-and-half until smooth. Bring the mixture to a boil over medium-high heat, stirring constantly. Lower the heat to maintain a simmer and cook, stirring constantly, 2 to 3 minutes.

3. Place the egg yolks in a bowl and slowly whisk 1 cup of the hot cream into them. Pour the mixture back into the saucepan and cook over low heat, stirring constantly, until the mixture thickens and just begins to "steam," 4 to 5 minutes. Do not let boil.

4. Remove the pan from the heat and stir in the butter and vanilla until smooth. Strain through a fine-mesh sieve into a bowl, cover with plastic wrap directly on the surface, and cool on a wire rack. When cool, gently fold in the coconut. Chill for 1 hour.

5. Preheat the oven to 400 degrees F.

6. On a lightly floured surface, roll out the dough into a ⅛-inch-thick round and fit into the pie pan. Trim any excess dough and crimp the edges decoratively. With a fork, prick the bottom and sides of the dough. Set the pan in the freezer for 20 minutes.

7. Cover the dough with aluminum foil and line the foil with the pie weights. Bake the shell for 15 minutes. Lower the oven temperature to 350 degrees F. Remove the pie weights and foil, and bake the shell 15 minutes more. Cool on a wire rack while making the whipped cream.

Make the whipped cream:

8. Put the cream, sugar, and vanilla in a bowl and beat until thickened using the electric mixer on high speed.

Assemble the pie:

9. Pour the cooled custard into the cooled prebaked crust and smooth the top. Mound the whipped cream over the filling and sprinkle with the coconut and nuts. Chill for 2 hours before serving.

Colada Cream Pie

➤ Makes 12 servings ◄

This Caribbean-inspired cream pie uses lightened cream cheese instead of custard for the filling. There are a lot of different textures at work here—ripe banana, shredded coconut, and, last but not least, a marvelous thick trellis of drizzled melted chocolate over the top. To make the intricate design, we used a squirt bottle to pipe out the chocolate. You can also use a pastry bag fitted with a small plain tip or a small plastic storage bag with a corner snipped off.

➤ Equipment Needed: ★ 9-INCH PIE PAN ★ PIE WEIGHTS ★ ELECTRIC MIXER

❦ Crust:

1½ cups all-purpose flour
¼ teaspoon salt

8 tablespoons (1 stick) cold unsalted butter, cut into chunks
3 to 4 tablespoons ice water

♥ Filling:

³/₄ cup coconut-pineapple juice, frozen
    or canned

4 ripe bananas, sliced

8 tablespoons (1 stick) unsalted butter,
    softened

16 ounces cream cheese, softened

2 cups sifted powdered sugar

¼ cup sour cream

2 tablespoons pure vanilla extract

1 cup shredded sweetened coconut,
    lightly toasted (see Tip: Toasting
    Coconut, page 21)

♥ Garnish:

½ cup chopped pecans, toasted

2 ounces semisweet chocolate, melted (see
    How to Melt Chocolate, page 18)

Make the crust:

1. In a bowl, whisk together the flour and salt. With a pastry cutter, cut in the butter until the mixture is coarsely textured with small, irregular flakes and bits the size of small peas. Sprinkle on the water, 1 tablespoon at a time, stirring with a fork until the dough just holds together. Gather the dough into a ball, flatten it into a disk, wrap it in plastic wrap, and chill for 1 hour.

2. On a lightly floured surface, roll out the dough into a ⅛-inch-thick round. Fit the dough into the pie pan, trim any excess dough, crimp the edges, and prick the bottom and sides with the tines of a fork. Set the shell in the freezer for 20 minutes.

3. Preheat the oven to 425 degrees F.

4. Cover the dough with aluminum foil and line the foil with the pie weights. Bake the shell for 15 minutes. Lower the oven temperature to 350 degrees F., remove the weights and foil, and bake 15 minutes more. Remove from the oven and cool on a wire rack.

Make the filling:

5. In a small shallow bowl, combine the juice and bananas for 5 minutes. Drain well, reserving the juice.

6. Put the butter and cream cheese in a bowl and beat until smooth using the electric mixer on medium speed. Add the sugar and beat until smooth. Scrape down the bowl. Add the sour cream, vanilla, and half of the reserved pineapple juice, and beat until combined. Cover the bowl with plastic wrap and chill until it is time to assemble the pie.

Assemble the pie:

7. Spread half of the cream cheese filling over the bottom of the prebaked shell and top with half of the bananas, arranging them in a single layer. Sprinkle the coconut over the bananas, then top the coconut with the remaining bananas. Spread the remaining cream cheese filling evenly and smoothly over the top of the pie.

Garnish:

8. Arrange the pecans over the cream cheese filling. Drizzle the melted chocolate over the top of the pie in a decorative pattern. Let the chocolate set before serving.

Debbi's Perfect Pecan Pie

➤ Makes 12 servings ◄

I admit that it's hard to claim to possess the perfect pecan pie recipe, especially since this classic American pie summons up such deep feelings. Everyone feels their family recipe is the best. Regardless, a great pecan pie is always worth eating, and here's the way I love mine: not too sweet, loaded with pecans, and touched with a whisper of bourbon. I serve it with a premium vanilla ice cream. See if my rendition doesn't come close to your idea of a perfect pecan pie.

➤ *Equipment Needed:* ★ 9-INCH PIE PLATE ★ ELECTRIC MIXER

♥ Crust:

1½ cups all-purpose flour

¼ teaspoon salt

8 tablespoons (1 stick) cold unsalted butter, cut into chunks

3 to 4 tablespoons ice water

♥ Filling:

6 tablespoons (¾ stick) unsalted butter, softened

1 cup firmly packed dark brown sugar

3 large eggs, at room temperature

¾ cup dark corn syrup

1 tablespoon pure vanilla extract

1 tablespoon bourbon

½ teaspoon salt

2½ cups pecan halves, toasted

Softened ice cream, as an accompaniment

Make the crust:

1. In a bowl, whisk together the flour and salt. With a pastry cutter, cut in the butter until the mixture is coarsely textured with small, irregular flakes and bits the size of small peas. Sprinkle on the water, 1 tablespoon at a time, stirring with a fork until the dough just holds together. Gather the dough into a ball, flatten it into a disk, wrap it in plastic wrap, and chill for 1 hour.

2. On a lightly floured surface, roll out the dough into a $\frac{1}{8}$-inch-thick round and fit into the pie pan. Trim any excess dough and crimp the edges decoratively. Set the pan in the freezer for 30 minutes.

3. Preheat the oven to 375 degrees F.

Make the filling:

4. Put the butter and sugar in a bowl and cream together using the electric mixer on medium speed. Add the eggs, 1 at a time, beating for 20 seconds after each addition. Scrape down the bowl. Add the corn syrup, vanilla, bourbon, and salt, and beat until combined. Fold in 1 cup of the pecans.

5. Pour the filling into the shell, then arrange the remaining $1\frac{1}{2}$ cups pecans over the filling. Bake for 55 to 60 minutes, until the center is no longer runny. (The filling will still be soft but will firm up with cooling.) Remove the pie to a wire rack to cool for 1 hour. Chill the pie for 2 hours.

6. To serve, cut the pie with a very sharp knife and top with softened ice cream.

Chocolate Rum Pecan Pie

≽ *Makes 12 servings* ≼

*S*ome people will tell you that there is only one pecan pie—the southern classic made with dark corn syrup and lots of pecans. As much as I love a traditional pecan pie, here's another one that rivals it in my affections because it's filled with chocolate! A chocolate layer covers the bottom crust, and there's melted chocolate in the filling. Even if you're a traditionalist, this is a very hard pie not to like. For a change of pace, serve it at Thanksgiving. You may be breaking with tradition, but you may also be starting a tradition of your own!

≽ *Equipment Needed:* ★ 9-INCH DEEP-DISH PIE PAN ★ ELECTRIC MIXER

₩ Crust:

1 1/2 cups all-purpose flour

1/4 teaspoon salt

8 tablespoons (1 stick) cold unsalted butter, cut into chunks

3 to 4 tablespoons ice water

₩ Filling:

3/4 cup firmly packed dark brown sugar

4 tablespoons (1/2 stick) unsalted butter, softened

4 large eggs, at room temperature

6 ounces semisweet chocolate, melted

1/2 cup dark corn syrup

2 tablespoons dark rum

1 tablespoon pure vanilla extract

2 tablespoons all-purpose flour

8 ounces pecan halves, toasted (see Tip, page 96)

6 ounces semisweet chocolate, cut into chunks

₩ Garnish:

Whipped cream

Make the crust:

1. In a bowl, whisk together the flour and salt. With a pastry cutter, cut in the butter until the mixture is coarsely textured with small, irregular flakes and bits the size of small peas. Sprinkle on the water, 1 tablespoon at a time, stirring with a fork until the dough just holds together. Gather the dough into a ball, flatten it into a disk, wrap in plastic wrap, and chill for 1 hour.
2. On a lightly floured surface, roll out the dough into a ⅛-inch-thick round. Fit the dough into the pie pan, trim any excess dough, crimp the edges decoratively, and prick the bottom and sides with the tines of a fork. Freeze the dough for 30 minutes.
3. Preheat the oven to 350 degrees F.

Make the filling:

4. Put the sugar and butter in a bowl and beat until fluffy, 4 to 5 minutes, using the electric mixer on medium speed. Add the eggs, 1 at a time, beating for 20 seconds after each addition. Scrape down the bowl. Add the melted chocolate and then the corn syrup, rum, and vanilla, beating until combined. Fold in the flour and pecans until combined.
5. Scatter the chocolate chunks evenly over the chilled shell. Pour in the filling.
6. Bake the pie on the middle rack of the oven for 45 to 50 minutes, until the center of the pie is no longer runny. (The pie will still be slightly jiggly when gently shaken.) Remove the pie to a wire rack and cool to room temperature. Chill the pie for 2 hours.
7. Serve the pie with generous dollops of whipped cream.

➤ *Tip:* STORING PECANS

Pecans are among my favorite nuts, and I use them often. Because they're highly perishable, I always store them in an airtight container in the freezer, where they stay fresh for up to six months.

Toasted Macadamia Nut Pie

During a family vacation in Hawaii, I discovered macadamia nuts and fell in love with them. I tried them in just about everything I baked, and discovered that with macadamias, you just can't go wrong. They add a rich, exotic buttery crunch to any recipe. Just try this Toasted Macadamia Nut Pie, which combines the best features of the two preceding pecan pies and these exotic Hawaiian nuts.

The key to the pie's success rests on the consistency of the caramel: too thin, and the caramel runs; too thick, and you won't be able to get the pie out of the pan! I'd advise erring on the side of making your caramel a little too thin. It will firm up when you refrigerate the pie. I'd suggest serving directly from the refrigerator to guarantee the best texture.

≽ *Equipment Needed:* ★ 8-INCH-SQUARE TART PAN WITH REMOVABLE BOTTOM ★ PASTRY BRUSH

♥ Crust:

2 cups chocolate wafer cookie crumbs

¼ cup sugar

8 tablespoons (1 stick) unsalted butter, melted

♥ Caramel:

2 tablespoons unsalted butter

½ cup heavy cream

¾ cup sugar

¼ cup water

1 teaspoon fresh lemon juice

♥ Chocolate Cream:

8 ounces semisweet chocolate, coarsely chopped

½ cup heavy cream

♥ Garnish:

1 cup coarsely chopped macadamia nuts, toasted

1. Preheat the oven to 375 degrees F.

Make the crust:

2. In a bowl, whisk together the wafer crumbs and sugar. Stir in the butter until combined. Press the crust over the bottom and up the sides of the tart pan. Bake for 9 minutes. Set aside to cool.

Make the caramel:

3. In a small ceramic or glass bowl covered with plastic wrap, heat the butter with the cream on High in a microwave oven for 30 seconds, or until the mixture is hot.
4. In a heavy saucepan over medium heat, combine the sugar, water, and lemon juice, stirring constantly until the sugar dissolves. With a pastry brush dipped in cold water, brush down the sides of the pan to remove any sugar crystals. Increase the heat to medium-high and cook the mixture, swirling the pan occasionally, until it turns a rich caramel color, about 10 minutes.
5. Quickly remove the pan from the heat and slowly pour in the heated cream mixture. Be careful—the mixture will boil rapidly. Return the pan to medium heat and stir the mixture with a wooden spoon until smooth. Lower the heat to a simmer and cook the caramel until it heavily coats the back of the spoon, 5 to 7 minutes. Remove the pan from the heat and keep the caramel warm.
6. Pour the warm caramel over the prebaked crust and smooth it into an even layer. Chill for 30 minutes.

Make the chocolate cream:

7. In a ceramic or glass bowl covered with plastic wrap, heat the chocolate with the cream, on High in a microwave oven for 30-second intervals, stirring after each interval, until smooth. Keep warm.
8. Pour the warm chocolate cream over the caramel in the crust and smooth into an even layer. Sprinkle the chopped macadamia nuts over the top. Let the pie cool to room temperature, then chill it until it is time to serve.
9. To serve, remove the sides of the tart pan and transfer the tart to a serving plate.

Debbi's Chocolate Cream Pie

*T*his pie is the best kind of old-fashioned cream pie, made with hand-rolled pastry, thick and creamy pudding, and clouds of fresh whipped cream. Don't be surprised if the chocolate filling disappears before you've had a chance to fill the shell—that's how dark and delicious it is! If you want to garnish the pie, chocolate curls look pretty on top.

➤ *Equipment Needed:* ★ 9-INCH DEEP-DISH PIE PAN ★ PIE WEIGHTS ★ ELECTRIC MIXER

❦ Pastry:

1½ cups all-purpose flour

¼ teaspoon salt

8 tablespoons (1 stick) cold unsalted butter, cut into tablespoons

1 large egg yolk, at room temperature

2 to 3 tablespoons ice water

❦ Filling:

1 cup sugar

¼ cup cornstarch

¼ teaspoon salt

2½ cups half-and-half

4 large egg yolks, at room temperature

4 tablespoons (½ stick) unsalted butter, cut into pieces

2 teaspoons pure vanilla extract

4 ounces unsweetened chocolate, chopped

❦ Whipped cream:

2 cups heavy cream, chilled

¼ cup powdered sugar

2 teaspoons pure vanilla extract

Make the pastry:

1. In a medium bowl, whisk together the flour and salt. With a pastry cutter, cut in the butter until the mixture is coarsely textured with small, irregular flakes and bits the size of small peas.

2. Lightly combine the yolk and 2 tablespoons ice water, and stir it into the dough with a fork. Add additional ice water, by the tablespoon, until the dough forms a ball. Flatten the dough into a disk, wrap it tightly in plastic wrap, and refrigerate it for 30 minutes.

3. On a floured surface, roll out the dough into a ⅛-inch-thick round. Fit the dough into the pie pan and crimp the edges decoratively. Prick the bottom and sides of the dough with a fork. Chill the dough in the freezer for 20 minutes.

4. Preheat the oven to 425 degrees F.

5. Cover the shell with aluminum foil and line the foil with pie weights. Bake the shell for 18 minutes. Lower the oven temperature to 350 degrees F., remove the weights and foil, and bake 15 minutes more, until the crust turns a light golden brown. Remove the pan to a wire rack and let cool to room temperature.

Make the filling:

6. In a heavy, medium-size saucepan, whisk together the sugar, cornstarch, and salt. Slowly stir in the half-and-half until smooth. Bring the mixture to a boil over medium-high heat, stirring constantly. Lower the heat to maintain a simmer and cook the mixture for 2 to 3 minutes.

7. In a bowl, lightly whisk the egg yolks. Pour the hot cream mixture slowly over them and whisk to combine. Pour the mixture back into the saucepan and cook over low heat, stirring constantly, until the cream thickens and just begins to "steam," 3 to 4 minutes. Do not let the mixture boil. It should heavily coat the back of the spoon and a finger drawn across the back of the spoon leaves a distinct line.

8. Remove the pan from the heat and stir in the butter, vanilla, and chocolate until smooth. Pour the pastry cream through a fine-mesh sieve into a bowl. Cover with plastic wrap directly on the surface to prevent a skin from forming, and let cool to room temperature.

Assemble the pie:

9. Pour the filling into the cooled crust. Cover the pie with plastic wrap and chill it thoroughly for at least 2 hours or overnight.

10. Before serving, make the whipped cream. Put the cream, sugar, and vanilla in a bowl and beat, using the electric mixer and chilled beaters, until stiff peaks form. Spoon the whipped cream over the filling and serve the pie immediately.

Ladyfinger Chocolate Meringue Pie

*D*esserts with the greatest appeal to me have complementary but contrasting textures. In this extravagant pie there are four different ones at play: the wonderful sponginess of a ladyfinger crust; the layer of melted chocolate that seals the crust; a soft, yielding filling of chocolate pastry cream; and on top of it all the airiness of meringue.

➤ *Equipment Needed:* ★ 9-INCH SPRINGFORM PAN ★ ELECTRIC MIXER

9 ounces store-bought ladyfingers (1 1/2 packages)   *8 ounces semisweet chocolate, coarsely chopped*

❦ Pastry cream:

1 1/4 cups sugar

1/4 cup cornstarch

1/2 cup unsweetened cocoa powder

Pinch of salt

2 cups half-and-half

6 large egg yolks, at room temperature

4 tablespoons (1/2 stick) unsalted butter,
   cut into pieces

1 tablespoon pure vanilla extract

❦ Meringue:

4 large egg whites, at room temperature

1/4 teaspoon cream of tartar

1/2 cup sugar

1. Spray the springform pan with nonstick cooking spray.
2. Cut the ladyfingers in half horizontally and arrange them around the sides of the pan, with rounded ends up and smooth sides facing in. Arrange the remaining ladyfingers over the bottom of the pan, filling in any gaps with small pieces.
3. In the top of a double boiler set over simmering water, melt the semisweet chocolate, stirring until smooth. Spread the chocolate over the ladyfingers in the bottom of the pan to seal the bottom crust. Set the pan aside.

Make the pastry cream:

4. In a medium-size saucepan, whisk together the sugar, cornstarch, cocoa powder, and salt. Slowly stir in the half-and-half until smooth. Place the pan over medium-high heat and bring the mixture to a boil, stirring constantly. Lower the heat to maintain a simmer and cook, stirring constantly, 2 to 3 minutes.

5. In a bowl, lightly whisk the egg yolks. Slowly pour ¼ cup of the hot cocoa mixture over the egg yolks and whisk to combine. Return the mixture to the pan and cook over low heat, stirring constantly and being sure to stir the bottom and sides of the pan, for 2 to 3 minutes more, or until the mixture thickens and heavily coats the back of a spoon. Do not let the mixture boil.

6. Remove the pan from the heat. Stir in the butter and vanilla until smooth. Strain the pastry cream through a fine-mesh sieve into a bowl, and cover with plastic wrap directly on the surface to prevent a skin from forming, and cool to room temperature. Chill until cold, about 1 hour.

7. Preheat the oven to 425 degrees F.

Make the meringue:

8. Put the egg whites in a bowl and beat until frothy using an electric mixer on medium speed. Add the cream of tartar and beat until soft peaks form. Gradually add the sugar and beat until stiff peaks form.

Assemble and bake the pie:

9. Pour the chilled pastry cream into the ladyfinger-and-chocolate-lined pan. With a spatula, spread the meringue over the pastry cream, extending it to touch the ladyfingers and swirling it decoratively.

10. Bake the pie for 6 to 8 minutes, until the meringue is a light golden brown. Remove the pie to a wire rack to cool for 30 minutes to 1 hour. Serve warm or refrigerate for about 1 hour and serve chilled.

➤ On Beating Egg Whites ◀

For maximum volume, beat egg whites that are at room temperature. If you want to warm eggs up in a hurry, place them in a bowl and pour hot tap water over them to cover. Let stand 15 to 20 minutes.

Even the slightest amount of yolk in the whites will prevent the whites from reaching full volume when beaten.

To ensure a perfect bowl of whites for beating, pour each white into its own custard cup, then add it to the larger bowl of egg whites. Should the white have yolk attached, all you have to do is throw out that white. If you had added it directly to the bowl, you'd be throwing out all the whites.

Pure egg whites can be frozen up to three months. Pour them into ice cube trays and freeze, then remove the cubes and store in freezer bags. Thaw frozen whites in the refrigerator and use immediately after thawing.

The bowl in which you beat egg whites can make a big difference in how stiff the whites become. Copper reacts chemically with the whites for maximum volume. A stainless-steel bowl is the next best thing. Avoid plastic bowls.

Debbi's Lemon Meringue Pie

*I*t's not easy to take a classic like lemon meringue pie and make it any better than it already is, but *my* lemon meringue pie has a very special crust. The crust combines lemon cookie crumbs for more lemon flavor with Grape-Nuts cereal for added crunch.

Remember that lemons, unlike oranges and grapefruits, are most available in the summer, which happens to be the perfect season for this lovely pie.

⪼ *Equipment Needed:* ★ 9-INCH DEEP-DISH PIE PAN ★ ELECTRIC MIXER

❦ Crust:

1½ cups lemon snap cookie crumbs (about 36 cookies, 1½ inches in diameter)

½ cup Grape-Nuts cereal

2 tablespoons powdered sugar

4 tablespoons (½ stick) unsalted butter, melted

❦ Filling:

1 cup sugar

¼ cup cornstarch

1½ cups water

½ cup fresh lemon juice

4 large egg yolks

1 tablespoon finely grated fresh lemon peel (see Tip: Grating Citrus Fruits, page 159)

4 tablespoons (½ stick) unsalted butter

❦ Meringue:

6 large egg whites, at room temperature

¼ teaspoon cream of tartar

½ cup sugar

❦ Garnish:

1 teaspoon finely grated fresh lemon peel

1. Preheat the oven to 350 degrees F.

Make the crust:
2. In a bowl, whisk the cookie crumbs, Grape-Nuts, and sugar, and stir in the butter until the mixture holds together. Press the crumbs over the bottom and up the sides of the pie pan. Bake the crust for 10 minutes. Cool on a wire rack.

Make the filling:
3. In a heavy-bottomed saucepan, combine the sugar and cornstarch. Add the water and lemon juice, and stir until smooth. Bring to a boil over medium-high heat, stirring constantly. Lower the heat to maintain a simmer and cook, stirring, until thickened, about 5 minutes. Whisk the egg yolks lightly in a heatproof bowl and slowly pour 1 cup of the hot mixture over them, stirring constantly. Pour the egg mixture back into the saucepan and cook over low heat, stirring until the mixture just steams. Remove the pan from the heat, stir in the peel and butter until thoroughly combined. Transfer the mixture to a bowl and cover loosely. Place on a wire rack to cool to room temperature.
4. Increase the oven temperature to 425 degrees F.

Make the meringue:
5. Beat the egg whites until frothy using the electric mixer on medium speed. Add the cream of tartar. Increase the speed to high and gradually beat in the sugar, a little at a time, until stiff peaks form.

Assemble the pie:
6. Pour the cooled lemon filling over the crust, spooning it evenly on the surface and then spreading it smooth. Spoon the meringue over the filling, making sure it extends to the edges of the crust, and swirl it decoratively into peaks.
7. Bake the pie for 6 to 8 minutes, or until the meringue is golden brown. Remove the pie to a wire rack to cool for 30 minutes, then chill it for 2 hours.
8. Before serving, sprinkle the lemon peel over the meringue.

Paradise Key Lime Pie

*T*he limes of the Florida Keys are famous, and so is the pie that is made from their special extra-tart juice. Many a traditional Key lime pie is made with sweetened condensed milk, which contributes a wonderful creamy texture that's offset by an airy crown of meringue.

I've used heavy cream instead of condensed milk and added macadamia nuts to the traditional pastry crust and covered it all with a cloud of meringue. If anyone tells you that a Key lime pie can be made with the juice of the Persian lime, you should reply, "Of course, but then it won't be Key lime pie!"

⇒ *Equipment Needed:*   ★   9-INCH DEEP-DISH PIE PAN   ★   PIE WEIGHTS
★   ELECTRIC MIXER

❦ Crust:

1 cup all-purpose flour

1/2 teaspoon salt

4 tablespoons (1/2 stick) cold unsalted butter, cut into pieces

3/4 cup toasted macadamia nuts, finely chopped

2 to 3 tablespoons ice water

❦ Filling:

1 cup sugar

1/4 cup cornstarch

1/4 teaspoon salt

1 1/2 cups heavy cream

3 large egg yolks

1/4 cup Key lime juice

1 tablespoon finely grated fresh lime peel (see Tip: Grating Citrus Fruits, page 159)

2 tablespoons unsalted butter

❦ Meringue:

4 large egg whites, at room temperature

1/4 teaspoon cream of tartar

1/2 cup sugar

❦ Garnish:

Lime curls

Make the crust:

1. In a bowl, whisk together the flour and salt. With a pastry cutter, cut in the butter until the mixture is coarsely textured with small, irregular flakes and bits the size of small peas. Stir in the nuts until combined. Sprinkle on the water, 1 tablespoon at a time, stirring with a fork until the dough just holds together. Gather the dough into a ball, flatten into a disk, wrap in plastic wrap, and refrigerate for 1 hour.

2. On a lightly floured surface, roll out the dough into a ⅛-inch-thick round. Fit the dough into the pie pan and crimp the edges decoratively. Prick the bottom and sides of the dough with a fork. Freeze the shell for 20 minutes.

3. Preheat the oven to 425 degrees F.

4. Cover the shell with aluminum foil and line the foil with the pie weights. Bake the shell for 15 minutes. Lower the oven temperature to 350 degrees F., remove the weights and foil, and bake 15 minutes more, until light golden brown in color. Remove to a rack and cool to room temperature.

Make the filling:

5. In a heavy-bottomed saucepan, whisk together the sugar, cornstarch, and salt. Slowly stir in the cream until smooth. Bring the mixture to a boil over medium-high heat, stirring constantly. Turn the heat to low to maintain a simmer and cook until thickened, 2 to 3 minutes. Slowly whisk 1 cup of the hot cream into the egg yolks in a bowl until smooth. Pour the mixture back into the saucepan and cook over low heat, stirring constantly, until the mixture just begins to "steam." Do not let it boil. Remove the pan from the heat and stir in the lime juice, peel, and butter until smooth. Pour the filling into a bowl, loosely cover, and cool on a wire rack to room temperature.

6. Increase the oven temperature to 425 degrees F.

Make the meringue:

7. Put the egg whites in a bowl and using an electric mixer on medium speed, beat until frothy. Add the cream of tartar, increase the speed to high, and gradually beat in the sugar, a little at a time, until stiff peaks form.

Assemble the pie:

8. Pour the cooled filling into the prebaked crust, spreading it evenly. Spoon the meringue over the filling, making sure it extends to the edges of the crust, and swirl it into decorative peaks.

9. Bake the pie for 6 to 8 minutes, until the meringue is golden. Remove the pie to a wire rack and cool for 30 minutes. Chill for 2 hours before serving.

10. Before serving, scatter the lime curls over the meringue.

Chapter 5

Old-Fashioned Desserts

PANDOWDY AND PUDDING, shortcake and cobbler, jelly roll and upside-down cake. These old-fashioned desserts are American treasures.

These are the kinds of desserts that were put together at the end of the afternoon when dinner was cooking on the back of the stove, and Mom realized a sweet was still needed for dessert. It had to be something simple, something that was made with ingredients that were in the larder.

Sometimes it took the form of bread pudding or custard. Those were easy to make because three things always on hand back then were bread, milk, and eggs.

Pandowdies and cobblers were simply variations on the great American dessert, apple pie. The earliest pandowdies included simply spiced apples topped with a biscuit or pie dough and baked. Cobblers, named either because of the way they were hurriedly put together or because of the way the biscuits looked on top—like cobblestones—were another well-liked colonial dessert.

My interpretations of the classic jelly roll, strawberry shortcake, and upside-down cake respect the original recipes and then embellish them in a way that I think you'll find delicious, too.

I've chosen these traditional desserts because of the fond memories they evoke. I love strawberry shortcake because we had it every year on my sister Cathy's birthday. I chose Pineapple Upside-Down Cake because my mother, who didn't bake often, always made this for me and my four sisters, and the aroma reminds me of the fun we all shared at the table.

Debbi's Banana Pudding

*T*here are reasons why custard pudding has remained popular for so long. It's very easy to like! It's simple to make and uses a few readily available ingredients. On its own, it's sweet and smooth and comforting. It can be used as a fast filling for pies or tarts if company is coming. Or you can layer it between cookies and soft ripe bananas, which is what I've done. And while plain vanilla—pudding, that is—is nice, it's more exciting when you add the tang of lemon. And don't forget some meringue on top, my final touch.

Pudding's reputation may have originally been as a homey, unassuming type of dessert—the kind that was served to family and friends. This rendition, which doesn't take that much more effort to make, can be served to family, friends, and guests.

≽ *Equipment Needed:* ★ 2½-QUART BAKING DISH ★ ELECTRIC MIXER

₩ Pastry cream:

⅔ cup sugar

¼ cup cornstarch

¼ teaspoon salt

2½ cups half-and-half

6 large egg yolks, at room temperature

1 tablespoon pure vanilla extract, divided into 2 teaspoons and 1 teaspoon

2 tablespoons fresh lemon juice

1 teaspoon grated fresh lemon peel (see Tip: Grating Citrus Fruits, page 159)

₩ Meringue:

6 large egg whites, at room temperature

¾ cup sugar

¼ teaspoon cream of tartar

40 vanilla wafer cookies, for layering

40 lemon snap cookies, for layering

6 medium bananas, for layering

Make the pastry cream:

1. In a heavy, medium-size saucepan, whisk together the sugar, cornstarch, and salt. Slowly stir in the half-and-half until smooth. Place the pan over medium-high heat and cook, stir-

ring constantly, until the mixture begins to boil. Lower the heat to maintain at a simmer and cook, stirring, for 2 to 3 minutes.

2. In a bowl, lightly whisk the egg yolks. Slowly pour half of the hot cream mixture over the yolks and whisk to combine. Return the mixture to the pan and cook it over low heat, stirring constantly and being sure to stir the bottom and sides of the pan for about 5 minutes, until the cream thickens and just starts to "steam." Do not let it boil. It should heavily coat the back of the spoon.

3. Remove the pan from the heat. Stir in 2 teaspoons of the vanilla and lemon juice. Strain the pastry cream through a fine-mesh sieve into a bowl, stir in the lemon peel, and place the bowl on a rack to cool to room temperature, stirring occasionally to prevent a skin from forming. Cover the bowl and chill it for about 1 hour, or until cold.

4. Preheat the oven to 425 degrees F. Butter the baking dish.

Assemble the pudding:

5. Cover the bottom of the prepared baking dish with a layer of vanilla cookies and a layer of lemon cookies, using a third of the cookies in all. Line the sides of the dish with vanilla cookies.

6. Slice 2 of the bananas and arrange them over the wafers; top the bananas with a third of the chilled pastry cream. Make 2 more layers with the remaining cookies, bananas, and pastry cream, ending with a layer of pastry cream.

Make the meringue:

7. Put the egg whites in a bowl and beat until frothy using the electric mixer on medium speed. Add the cream of tartar and beat until stiff peaks form. Slowly beat in the sugar until stiff peaks form. Fold the remaining 1 teaspoon vanilla in gently. Spread the meringue over the pastry cream, sealing the edges to the rim of the dish.
8. Place the pudding in the oven for 6 to 8 minutes, or until the meringue is golden brown. Remove the dish from the oven to a wire rack to cool for 10 minutes, then refrigerate it for 3 to 4 hours before serving.

Chocolate Banana Pudding

➤ *Makes 12 servings* ◄

*T*he flavors of good chocolate and ripe, sweet bananas were made for each other, so I decided to combine them. Pieces of light chocolate cake (the same one that's used in Baby Baked Alaskas, page 211) are layered between smooth pastry cream and slices of bananas, with sweetened whipped cream over all. Just the description of it sounds indulgent and delicious, and it is.

See Tip: Making Desserts in Stages and Ripening Bananas, page 116, for how to go about making the various parts of this luscious and comforting dessert in advance.

➤ *Equipment Needed:* ★ 3-QUART SERVING BOWL ★ ELECTRIC MIXER

1 chocolate sheet cake, baked and cooled
   according to the directions on page 212

♥ Pastry cream:

1 cup sugar

¹/₄ cup cornstarch

¹/₄ teaspoon salt

2¹/₂ cups half-and-half

4 large egg yolks

4 ounces unsweetened chocolate, chopped

4 tablespoons (¹/₂ stick) unsalted butter, cut into
   chunks

2 teaspoons pure vanilla extract

♥ Whipped cream:

2 cups heavy cream, chilled

¹/₄ cup powdered sugar

2 teaspoons pure vanilla extract

6 medium bananas, for layering

Make the pastry cream while the sheet cake is baking and cooling:

1. In a medium-size heavy saucepan, whisk together the sugar, cornstarch, and salt. Slowly stir in the half-and-half until smooth. Place the pan over medium-high heat and cook, stirring constantly, until the mixture begins to boil. Lower the heat to keep the mixture at a simmer and cook, stirring, 2 to 3 minutes.

2. In a bowl, lightly whisk the egg yolks. Slowly pour 1 cup of the hot cream mixture over the yolks and whisk to combine. Return the mixture to the pan and cook it over low heat, stirring constantly until thickened and just starts to "steam," 4 to 5 minutes. Do not let it boil. It should heavily coat the back of the spoon.

3. Remove the pan from the heat. Stir in the chopped chocolate, butter, and vanilla until combined. Strain the pastry cream through a fine-mesh sieve into a bowl and place the bowl on a rack to cool to room temperature, stirring occasionally to prevent a skin from forming. Cover and let chill.

Make the whipped cream:

4. Put the cream, sugar, and vanilla in a bowl and beat using an electric mixer on high speed until thickened.

Assemble the pudding:

5. Break half of the cake into pieces to fit the bottom of the serving bowl. Spread with half of the pastry cream. Top with slices from 3 of the bananas. Repeat the layers with the remaining cake, pastry cream, and bananas. Mound the top with whipped cream, then refrigerate the pudding for 2 hours before serving.

➤ *Tip:* MAKING DESSERT IN STAGES AND RIPENING BANANAS

You can make this dessert in stages. Make the pastry cream and refrigerate it overnight. The next day, bake the cake and assemble the dessert for serving.

Be sure that your bananas are at just the right stage of ripeness. Don't use ones that are too soft or darkened. And if the ones you have on hand are not quite ripe enough, simply put them in a plastic bag and seal it. The ethylene gas they give off will act to ripen them more quickly than if you left them out at room temperature to soften with time. Add an apple or pear to the bag; those fruits produce ethylene gas, too.

Debbi's Bread Pudding

➤ *Makes 12 servings* ◀

*R*andy can never pass up bread pudding. Ever. So this was the first dessert I learned to make when we got married. This is comfort food at its best—delicious and sweet and soothing—*and* it's easy to make! Bread pudding was originally a practical way of using up what remained of a loaf of bread by adding milk, sugar, and eggs. This is a much fancier version of the old-fashioned favorite.

If you really want to gild the lily, drizzle the pudding with pure maple syrup, after it has baked, then run the dish under the broiler for a minute or two. You can serve this with Apricot-Orange Sauce and while very tasty it *is* optional.

➤ *Equipment Needed:* ★ 3-QUART BAKING DISH   ★ ELECTRIC MIXER

2 tablespoons unsalted butter, softened (for
    greasing the dish)
4 cups heavy cream
¼ cup brandy
2 tablespoons pure vanilla extract
1 pound day-old French (or similar type)
    bread, cut into ¾-inch cubes

3 large eggs
1¼ cups sugar
½ cup dark raisins
½ cup golden raisins

♦ Topping:

1 cup pecan pieces, toasted
½ cup firmly packed light brown sugar
1 tablespoon ground cinnamon
2 tablespoons unsalted butter, melted

½ cup pure maple syrup (optional)
1 recipe Apricot-Orange Sauce (page 39), as an
    accompaniment

1. Preheat the oven to 325 degrees F. Butter the baking dish.
2. In a large bowl, combine the cream, brandy, and vanilla. Add the bread and stir to coat.
3. Put the eggs and sugar in a bowl and beat together until thickened using the electric mixer
   on medium speed. The mixture should drop in thick ribbons when the beaters are lifted
   from the bowl, about 5 minutes. Fold into the bread mixture, then add the raisins, folding
   them in gently. Transfer the pudding to the buttered dish.

Prepare the topping:
4. In a small bowl, mix the pecan pieces, brown sugar, cinnamon, and butter together until
   thoroughly combined.
5. Spread the topping evenly over the top of the pudding.
6. Place the baking dish on the middle rack of the oven. Set a larger baking pan filled with a
   few inches of hot water on the rack beneath. Bake for 55 to 60 minutes, until the pudding
   is set in the center. (It will still be slightly jiggly.) Remove the pudding to a wire rack to
   cool for 1 hour.
7. Before serving, drizzle with the maple syrup, if desired. Serve with the Apricot-Orange
   Sauce on the side.

Chocolatey Bread Pudding

Makes 5 servings

As soon as I pull this bread pudding out of the oven, Randy is lurking behind me with his fork, ready to dig in. If I'm lucky, I can get it into a serving dish before the whole pan becomes one serving . . . his! So if you think bread pudding is out of fashion, think again!

Equipment Needed: ★ FIVE 1½-CUP BAKING DISHES ★ ELECTRIC MIXER

2 tablespoons unsalted butter, softened (for greasing the dishes)

2 cups half-and-half or light cream

2 tablespoons dark rum

2 tablespoons pure vanilla extract

5 cups day-old French bread or similar bread, cut into ¾-inch squares

2 large eggs

½ cup sugar

12 ounces semisweet chocolate, melted and cooled slightly (see *How to Melt Chocolate*, page 18)

Grated semisweet chocolate, for garnish

Whipped cream, for garnish

1. Preheat the oven to 325 degrees F. Lightly butter the baking dishes.
2. In a large bowl, combine the half-and-half, rum, and vanilla. Add the bread and stir to coat.
3. Put the eggs and sugar in a bowl and cream together until fluffy using an electric mixer on medium speed, 4 or 5 minutes. Stir in the warm chocolate until smooth. Add the chocolate mixture to the bread mixture, folding it in with a rubber spatula until thoroughly combined.
4. Divide the mixture among the prepared baking dishes, then set the dishes in a baking pan large enough to hold them comfortably. Pour hot water into the larger pan to come halfway up the sides of the small dishes.
5. Set the pan on the middle rack of the oven and bake until the centers of the puddings are set, 30 to 35 minutes. Remove the pan to a wire rack to cool for 10 minutes, then take the dishes out of the pan and let cool.

6. Serve warm or at room temperature. If serving warm, garnish with grated chocolate and whipped cream. To serve chilled: Let the warm puddings cool to room temperature for 1 hour, then refrigerate for at least 2 hours before serving.

Raspberry Cream Jelly Roll

Makes 15 servings

What I like about old-fashioned jelly roll—besides the way it looks—is the number of ways you can fill it. Jelly or jam is the obvious choice, and I haven't departed too much from tradition here: I just added the jam to softly whipped cream!

A lovely light sheet cake is a must for jelly roll. Should it crack while you're rolling it, just sprinkle on a little extra powdered sugar or put a fresh berry or two over the split. The roll can, in fact, be assembled one day in advance of serving; wrap it securely in plastic wrap and chill in the refrigerator. And if you're making this on the spur of the moment, remember that softened ice cream is a great filling, too! You'll need about ¾ of a pint, and you should put the roll, wrapped in plastic wrap and foil, into the freezer for at least 2 hours before serving.

Equipment Needed: ★ 10 BY 15-INCH JELLY-ROLL PAN ★ ELECTRIC MIXER

Cake:

⅓ cup cake flour, sifted
2 tablespoons cornstarch
4 large eggs, at room temperature, separated
½ cup plus 1 tablespoon sugar
2 teaspoons pure vanilla extract
2 tablespoons unsalted butter, melted
¼ teaspoon cream of tartar

♥ Filling:

1 cup heavy cream, well chilled

1 cup seedless raspberry jam, divided

¼ cup powdered sugar, for dusting

1. Preheat the oven to 400 degrees F. Line the jelly-roll pan with foil, and butter and flour the foil.

Make the cake:

2. In a bowl, whisk together the cake flour and cornstarch.
3. Put the egg yolks in a bowl and beat using the electric mixer on medium-high speed. Slowly add the ½ cup sugar and beat until light and fluffy, about 5 minutes. Add the vanilla and melted butter and beat on low speed until smooth. Scrape down the bowl.
4. Sift the flour mixture over the yolk mixture in 2 batches, folding it in thoroughly after each addition.

5. Put the egg whites in a bowl and beat until frothy using the electric mixer on high speed and clean beaters. Add the cream of tartar and beat until soft peaks form. Add the remaining 1 tablespoon sugar and beat until stiff peaks form. Add $\frac{1}{3}$ of the beaten whites to the batter, folding it in thoroughly to lighten it. Add the remaining whites, folding them in gently but thoroughly.

6. Scrape the batter into the prepared pan and bake on the middle rack of the oven for 8 to 12 minutes, until the top is golden brown and the center of the cake springs back when gently pressed. Transfer the pan to a wire rack, place a damp towel over the cake, and cool for 5 minutes. Remove the towel, transfer the cake on the foil to a flat surface, and let it cool. With a knife, gently loosen the edges of the cake from the foil if necessary.

Make the filling:

7. In a bowl, beat the cream until thickened, using the mixer with chilled beaters on high speed. Fold in $\frac{1}{2}$ cup raspberry jam.

8. In a small ceramic or glass bowl, microwave the remaining $\frac{1}{2}$ cup raspberry jam on High for 30 seconds, until warm. Stir until smooth.

Assemble the cake:

9. Spread the warm jam evenly over the cooled cake. Top with the filling, spreading it evenly and leaving a 1-inch border on the long sides. Facing a long side, roll up the cake, slowly removing the foil as you roll.

10. With 2 large, thin spatulas, transfer the cake, seam side down, to a serving platter. (Or cut in half and place the halves on a platter.) Dust with the powdered sugar before serving. Cut the cake into 1-inch slices with a sharp, thin knife.

Chocolate Cream Jelly Roll

*H*ere is an old-fashioned cake with a new-fashioned filling—a lovely, rich, smooth chocolate cream. Be patient beating the chocolate cream: You want to triple its volume for best texture. Warming the chocolate sauce that accompanies this crowd-pleasing dessert will add another elegant note.

➤ *Equipment Needed:* ★ 10 BY 15-INCH JELLY-ROLL PAN
                                       ★ ELECTRIC MIXER

▼ Chocolate cream:

¾ cup heavy cream

6 ounces sweet chocolate, chopped into small
    pieces

1 jelly-roll cake, the batter made according to
    the directions on page 119

½ cup powdered sugar

1 recipe Chocolate Sauce (page 41), for serving

Make the chocolate cream:

1. In a ceramic or glass bowl covered with plastic wrap, heat the cream with the chocolate on High in a microwave oven for 30-second intervals, stirring after each interval, until smooth. Cool to room temperature, stirring occasionally, for 1 hour.

2. While the chocolate mixture cools, bake the cake as directed on page 120, but before removing it from the oven, dust a kitchen towel with the powdered sugar. Remove the baked cake from the oven and cool on a rack for 5 minutes. Loosen the edges of the cake with a metal spatula, then invert the cake onto the sugar-dusted towel.

3. Set the bowl of chocolate cream in a larger bowl of ice water. With a large balloon whisk beat the mixture until it thickens and almost doubles in volume.

Assemble the cake:

4. Spread the chocolate cream filling over the cake, leaving a 1-inch border on the long sides. With a long edge of the cake facing you, carefully roll the cake into a cylinder, using the towel as a guide.

5. With 2 long, thin spatulas, transfer the cake to a serving platter. (Or cut in half and place the halves on a platter.) Cut the cake into 1-inch slices with a long, thin knife and serve with chocolate sauce.

Debbi's Strawberry Shortcake

*M*y strawberry shortcakes depart from the traditional—or perhaps I should say more expected—version of this great American classic dessert. Traditionally, sweetened homemade biscuits are split, the bottom halves are covered in sugared juicy strawberries, and the biscuits are put back together again, crowned with the top and lots of soft whipped cream.

I've added a few little variations. I've enriched the cookielike biscuits with pecans and brown sugar and piled the berries over pastry cream. Once topped, the biscuits become soft and incredibly yielding. And I always serve a few extra berries on the side to wipe up the last of the cream.

Assemble these shortcakes right before serving to ensure that the different flavors and textures remain distinct.

Equipment Needed: ★ ELECTRIC MIXER ★ BAKING SHEETS ★ 3-INCH COOKIE OR BISCUIT CUTTER

▼ Shortcake:

1½ cups all-purpose flour

¾ cup firmly packed dark brown sugar

1 tablespoon baking powder

¼ teaspoon salt

8 tablespoons (1 stick) cold unsalted butter, cut into tablespoons

½ cup chopped pecans, toasted

2 teaspoons pure vanilla extract

3 to 4 tablespoons milk

▼ Strawberries:

4 cups hulled sliced strawberries, plus additional strawberries for garnish

3 tablespoons sugar

1 tablespoon fresh lemon juice

❧ Pastry cream:

¹/₃ cup sugar

2 tablespoons cornstarch

Pinch of salt

1 cup half-and-half

3 large egg yolks

1 tablespoon unsalted butter

1¹/₂ teaspoons pure vanilla extract

❧ Whipped cream:

1 cup heavy cream, well chilled

2 tablespoons powdered sugar

1 teaspoon pure vanilla extract

1. Preheat the oven to 425 degrees F. Lightly butter or spray the baking sheets with nonstick cooking spray.

Make the shortcakes:

2. In a large bowl, whisk together the flour, brown sugar, baking powder, and salt. With a pastry cutter, cut in the butter until the mixture is coarsely textured with small, irregular flakes and bits the size of small peas. Stir in the nuts. Add the vanilla and sprinkle on the milk, 1 tablespoon at a time, and stir until the dough just holds together.

3. Gather the dough into a ball and on a lightly floured surface roll it out in a ½-inch-thick round. With a 3-inch cookie or biscuit cutter, cut out biscuits and place them 1 inch apart on a baking sheet. Gather the scraps of dough, reroll them, and cut out biscuits with this dough. You should have 10 rounds.

4. Bake the biscuits for 10 to 15 minutes, or until golden on top. Immediately transfer the biscuits from the pan to a wire rack to cool.

Prepare the strawberries:

5. In a large bowl, combine the strawberries, sugar, and lemon juice, and chill.

Make the pastry cream:

6. In a small, heavy saucepan, whisk together the sugar, cornstarch, and salt. Slowly stir in the half-and-half until smooth. Place the pan over medium-high heat and bring the mixture to a boil, stirring constantly. Lower the heat to maintain a simmer and continue cooking for 2 to 3 minutes, stirring constantly.

7. In a bowl, whisk together the egg yolks. Pour half of the hot cream mixture slowly over the yolks and whisk to combine. Pour the mixture back into the pan. Cook over low heat, stirring constantly, 3 to 4 minutes, until the pastry cream thickens and just begins to "steam." Do not let it boil. It should heavily coat the back of the spoon. Stir in the butter and vanilla until combined. Remove the pan from the heat and strain the hot cream through a fine-mesh sieve into a bowl. Cover with plastic wrap directly on the surface to prevent a skin from forming, then refrigerate until cold.

Make the whipped cream:

8. Put the cream, sugar, and vanilla in a chilled bowl and beat until stiff peaks form using the mixer on medium speed and chilled beaters.

Assemble the shortcakes:

9. Place 1 biscuit on a dessert plate and top with a generous spoonful of the pastry cream. Top with some of the strawberries and a second biscuit. Pipe or spoon a dollop of whipped cream on each shortcake and garnish with 1 or 2 sliced strawberries.

Strawberry-Peach Shortcake

➤ *Makes 12 servings* ≼

*H*ere is the classic baking powder dough shortcake biscuit that I've fashioned into one large biscuit and split. Once again I've used pastry cream for the filling, then topped it off with the lid of the biscuit, two luscious summer fruits, and lots of whipped cream.

Go ahead and make the parts of this dessert ahead of time. Prepare the pastry cream a day in advance and the biscuit earlier on the day of serving. Wait until serving, though, to bring all the pieces together.

If you're really pressed for time or don't want to use the pastry cream, prepare extra fruit and spoon it over the bottom of the biscuit. Top with the biscuit lid and lots of whipped cream. No matter how you prepare dessert, it's the most wonderful ending to a summertime meal. It's the perfect finish to a Fourth of July celebration especially if you use blueberries in place of the peaches.

➤ *Equipment Needed:* ★ 9-INCH CAKE PAN ★ BAKING PARCHMENT

❦ Shortcake:

2 cups all-purpose flour

½ cup sugar

1 tablespoon baking powder

½ teaspoon salt

8 tablespoons (1 stick) unsalted butter, melted

2 large eggs, at room temperature, lightly beaten

1 cup whole milk

2 teaspoons pure vanilla extract

❦ Fruit:

2 pints strawberries, hulled and sliced, with several slices reserved for garnish

2 cups sliced fresh peaches (about 4 medium)

¼ cup sugar

1 recipe Pastry Cream, cooled (page 125), as accompaniment

1 recipe Whipped Cream (page 125), for topping

1. Preheat the oven to 350 degrees F. Butter the cake pan, line it with baking parchment (or wax paper), and butter and flour the paper.

Make the shortcake:

2. In a large bowl, whisk together the flour, sugar, baking powder, and salt.
3. In another bowl, stir together the butter, eggs, milk, and vanilla. Pour the mixture over the dry ingredients and stir just to combine.
4. Pour the batter into the prepared pan and bake for 25 to 30 minutes, or until a toothpick inserted in the center comes out clean. Remove the pan to a wire rack and cool for 10 minutes. Turn the cake out of the pan and let it cool to room temperature. When cool, slice the cake horizontally in half.

Prepare the fruit:

5. In a large bowl, combine the strawberries and peaches with the sugar and chill.
6. Prepare the pastry cream and whipped cream.

Assemble the shortcake:

7. Place the bottom layer of the shortcake, cut side up, on a serving plate and spread it with the pastry cream. Top with half of the fruit. Arrange the remaining cake layer on top. Spoon the remaining fruit over the cake and mound with the whipped cream over all. Serve immediately.

Blackberry Cobbler

*C*obblers and pandowdies, both great American desserts, have much in common, each being a simple-to-prepare, homey combination of fruit and dough that is then baked into comforting deliciousness. Each has been likened to that other great American favorite—apple pie!

A cobbler was originally made according to what fruit was on hand at the time, most probably apples. We have the advantage of what used to be seasonal fruits almost year-round now, which means I can make this blackberry cobbler, my favorite of all, anytime.

➤ *Equipment Needed:* ★ 9 BY 13-INCH BAKING DISH

12 tablespoons (1½ sticks) unsalted but-
    ter, cut into tablespoons
1½ cups all-purpose flour
1½ cups sugar
2 teaspoons baking powder
½ teaspoon salt
1½ cups milk, at room temperature
1 teaspoon pure vanilla extract
3 cups fresh or frozen unsweetened
    whole blackberries (if frozen, thawed
    and well drained)

1. Preheat the oven to 350 degrees F.
   Place the butter in the baking dish
   and put the dish in the oven to melt
   the butter.

2. In a large bowl, whisk together the flour,
   sugar, baking powder, and salt. Stir in
   the milk and vanilla until combined.

3. Remove the hot baking dish from the oven and immediately pour the batter into it. Spoon the blackberries evenly over the batter. Return the hot dish to the oven and bake 40 to 45 minutes. Remove to a wire rack and cool. Serve warm or at room temperature.

Apple Pandowdy

➤ *Makes 8 servings* ◄

*T*he old-fashioned pandowdy was nothing more than apples baked under a tender biscuit crust. I've added a little something extra—a crumb topping with brown sugar and oats—for more texture. Some say that the name for this dessert came from the way it looks, but I want to point out there's nothing "dowdy" about this pandowdy at all!

In earlier times, pies, pandowdies, and similar desserts were often served for breakfast. Why not offer this treat to your family one crisp fall morning. It's a pandowdy that's worth jumping out of bed for!

➤ *Equipment Needed:* ★ 2-QUART BAKING DISH

❦ Filling:

4 cups peeled and sliced tart apples, such as
   Granny Smith (5 to 7 medium apples, see Tip,
   page 130)
½ cup honey

½ teaspoon ground cinnamon
½ teaspoon ground nutmeg
¼ teaspoon salt

❦ Dough:

1½ cups all-purpose flour
½ cup sugar
2 teaspoons baking powder
½ teaspoon salt

1 large egg, at room temperature, lightly beaten
½ cup milk
8 tablespoons (1 stick) unsalted butter, melted

❦ Crumb topping:

½ cup firmly packed light brown sugar

¼ cup all-purpose flour

½ cup quick oats (not instant, see Tip: Types of Oats, page 227)

4 tablespoons (½ stick) unsalted butter, melted

1. Preheat the oven to 350 degrees F. Butter the baking dish.

Make the filling:

2. Toss the apple slices in the prepared baking dish with the honey, cinnamon, nutmeg, and salt. Cover the pan with foil and bake 20 to 25 minutes, or until the apples are soft. Remove from the oven but keep covered.

Make the dough:

3. In a bowl, whisk together the flour, sugar, baking powder, and salt.
4. In another bowl, stir together the egg, milk, and melted butter. Pour over the dry ingredients and stir to combine.

Make the crumb topping:

5. In a bowl, stir together the brown sugar, flour, and oats until combined. Add the melted butter and mix well.

Assemble the dessert:

6. Place the dough on the apples, then sprinkle the crumb topping over the dough.
7. Bake 35 to 40 minutes, or until golden on the top. Transfer to a wire rack and let cool slightly. Serve warm.

➤ Tip: FAVORITE BAKING APPLES

Some of my other favorite baking apples are Winesap, Cortland, Rome Beauties, and Braeburns. And it's also fun to combine them.

Three-Fruit Pandowdy

➤ *Makes 6 servings* ◀

I've improved the old-fashioned, comforting one-fruit pandowdy using fresh pears, dried apricots and cherries, and a crunchy crumb topping. This is a great dessert to serve instead of pie. This dough is easy to prepare, easy to roll, and a breeze to fit into the pan. All you do to finish it is fold the edges over the fruit.

I like to serve this slightly warm, and I've been known to accompany it with heavy cream or even a bowlful of softened vanilla ice cream.

If you have any leftovers, remember that pandowdies and similar old-time fruit desserts often reappeared at breakfast the following day.

➤ *Equipment Needed:* ★ 8-INCH SQUARE BAKING DISH

♥ Dough:

1½ cups all-purpose flour

½ cup sugar

1½ teaspoons baking powder

½ teaspoon baking soda

¼ teaspoon salt

1 large egg, at room temperature, lightly beaten

½ cup buttermilk

4 tablespoons (½ stick) unsalted butter, melted

♥ Fruit filling:

1¼ cups sugar

3 tablespoons all-purpose flour

1 tablespoon ground cinnamon

¼ teaspoon ground nutmeg

¼ teaspoon salt

5 cups peeled and sliced ripe pears (4 to 5 medium)

½ cup coarsely chopped dried apricots

½ cup dried cherries

❦ Topping:

⅓ cup firmly packed light brown sugar

⅓ cup Grape-Nuts cereal

⅓ cup all-purpose flour

2 teaspoons pure vanilla extract

4 tablespoons (½ stick) unsalted butter, melted

❦ Eggwash:

1 large egg, at room temperature, beaten

1. Preheat the oven to 350 degrees F.

Make the dough:

2. In a medium-size bowl, whisk together the flour, sugar, baking powder, baking soda, and salt.

3. In a small bowl, whisk together the egg, buttermilk, and melted butter. Pour the mixture into the dry ingredients and combine with a wooden spoon until a ball of dough forms. Wrap the dough in plastic wrap and chill for 30 minutes.
4. On a lightly floured surface, roll the dough into a 12-inch square. Fit the dough into the baking pan, letting the extra dough fall loosely over the sides. Chill the pan.

Prepare the fruit:
5. In a bowl, combine the sugar, flour, cinnamon, nutmeg, salt, pears, apricots, and cherries, and toss to combine.

Make the crumb topping:
6. In a bowl, combine the sugar, Grape-Nuts, and flour. Add the vanilla and butter, and stir until combined.

Assemble the pandowdy:
7. Place the fruit on the chilled dough in the pan. Sprinkle with the crumb topping. Fold the sides of the dough over the fruit, partially covering the filling. Brush the dough with the eggwash.
8. Bake on the middle rack of the oven for 45 to 50 minutes, or until bubbly and golden. Transfer to a wire rack and cool slightly. Serve warm.

Pineapple Upside-Down Cake

≥ *Makes 12 servings* ≤

*P*ineapple in a can was "invented" at the beginning of the twentieth century. Until then, people who didn't live in or near pineapple-growing areas had to be content with reading about the wonders of this truly delicious tropical fruit or wait for someone to bring one back from atrip to one of their few exotic growing locales. Once pineapple in cans became widely available, people began to find more uses for the fruit, including, of course, pineapple upside-down cake.

What accounts for this cake's long-lasting charm? Several things: It has the most delicious brown sugar topping, and there is something fantastic about how the pineapple rings look. If some of the topping sticks, simply use a spatula to stick it back on!

≥ *Equipment Needed:* ★ 10-INCH CAKE PAN ★ ELECTRIC MIXER

❦ Topping:

6 tablespoons (¾ stick) unsalted butter

1 cup firmly packed brown sugar

1 tablespoon honey

2½ cups canned pineapple slices, drained with
   juice reserved (see Tip, page 137)

½ cup dried currants

¼ cup almond slices, toasted, plus additional
   for garnish, if desired

♥ Cake:

¹/₄ cup dark rum

¹/₄ cup pineapple juice (reserved from above) or
   fresh orange juice

¹/₄ cup buttermilk

1¹/₂ cups all-purpose flour

2 teaspoons baking powder

1 teaspoon ground cinnamon

¹/₄ teaspoon ground nutmeg

¹/₄ teaspoon salt

¹/₈ teaspoon ground cloves

6 tablespoons (³/₄ stick) unsalted butter, softened

1 cup firmly packed light brown sugar

2 large eggs, at room temperature

1 tablespoon pure vanilla extract

¹/₂ teaspoon pure almond extract

1. Preheat the oven to 350 degrees F.

Make the topping:

2. In a heavy-bottomed saucepan over medium heat, combine the butter, brown sugar, and honey, and stir until smooth. Pour into the baking pan, tilting it to cover the entire surface.

Arrange the pineapple slices, currants, and almonds in a decorative pattern in the sugar syrup. Set the pan aside.

Make the cake:

3. In a small bowl, combine the rum, pineapple juice, and buttermilk.
4. In a bowl, whisk together the flour, baking powder, cinnamon, nutmeg, salt, and cloves.
5. Put the butter and brown sugar in a bowl and cream together until fluffy, 4 to 5 minutes, using the electric mixer on medium speed. Add the eggs, 1 at a time, beating for 20 seconds after each addition. Scrape down the bowl. Beat in the vanilla and almond extracts, and scrape down the bowl again.
6. Add the dry ingredients to the sugar mixture in thirds, alternating with the rum-juice mixture. Beat for 45 seconds after each addition, and begin and end with the dry ingredients. Blend until well combined. Scrape down the bowl. Pour the batter over the fruit in the pan.
7. Bake for 35 to 40 minutes, or until a cake tester inserted in the cake, not the fruit, comes out with a few moist crumbs. Remove the cake to a wire rack and let stand for 10 minutes.
8. Place a serving plate over the baking pan and invert the pan. Let the cake rest, still in the pan, 10 minutes more before removing. With a spatula, remove any topping that may still remain in the pan. Before serving, garnish with additional almond slices, if desired.

➤ *Tip:* PINEAPPLE RINGS

You can make this with fresh ripe pineapple sliced into rings approximately ½ inch thick. Replace the pineapple juice that is called for in the batter with an equal amount of fresh orange juice.

Chocolate Pineapple Upside-Down Cake

*T*his cake has a decidedly tropical flavor. In addition to the pineapple I've added macadamia nuts and coconut. Close your eyes, take a bite, and imagine the Hawaiian Islands! And the cake itself is dark with cocoa powder and rich with the flavor of chocolate liqueur. You might not immediately think of putting chocolate and pineapple together, but the combination is very special. It's funny all the places that a love for chocolate can take you!

➤ *Equipment Needed:* ★ 9 BY 13-INCH BAKING PAN ★ ELECTRIC MIXER

♥ Topping:

1 cup firmly packed light brown sugar

6 tablespoons (¾ stick) unsalted butter

2 tablespoons pineapple juice (reserved from drained canned slices)

2½ cups canned pineapple slices, drained with

juices reserved (see Tip: Pineapple Rings, page 137)

1 cup macadamia nuts, toasted

¾ cup loosely packed shredded sweetened coconut

♥ Cake:

1¼ cups all-purpose flour

¼ cup unsweetened cocoa powder

2 teaspoons baking powder

¼ teaspoon salt

¼ cup reserved pineapple juice (from above)

¼ cup crème de cacao (chocolate-flavored liqueur)

¼ cup sour cream

1 tablespoon pure vanilla extract

8 tablespoons (1 stick) unsalted butter, softened

1 cup firmly packed light brown sugar

2 large eggs, at room temperature

Whipped cream (optional)

1. Preheat the oven to 350 degrees F.

Make the topping:

2. In a heavy-bottomed saucepan over medium heat, combine the brown sugar, butter, and pineapple juice, and cook, stirring until smooth and slightly thickened, about 10 minutes. Pour the syrup into the baking pan, tilting it to coat the surface evenly. Arrange the pineapple slices, macadamia nuts, and coconut in the sugar syrup in a decorative pattern. Set the pan aside.

Make the cake:

3. In a bowl, whisk together the flour, cocoa powder, baking powder, and salt. Set aside.
4. In a small bowl, combine the pineapple juice, crème de cacao, sour cream, and vanilla. Set aside.
5. Put the butter and brown sugar in a bowl and cream together until fluffy, 4 to 5 minutes, using an electric mixer on medium speed. Add the eggs, 1 at a time, beating for 20 seconds after each addition. Scrape down the bowl.
6. Add the dry ingredients to the butter mixture in thirds, alternating with the pineapple juice mixture. Beat for 45 seconds after each addition, and begin and end with the dry ingredients. Blend until well combined. Scrape down the bowl. Place the batter over the pineapple topping in the pan.
7. Bake for 35 to 40 minutes, or until the cake springs back when touched. Remove the cake from the oven to a wire rack and cool for 10 minutes.
8. Place a serving plate over the baking pan and invert the pan. (If the cake does not drop right out, let it stand, still in the pan, 10 minutes more before removing the cake pan.) Serve warm with whipped cream, if desired.

Debbi's Sweet Potato Pie

*S*weet potato, yam, or even squash pie is a regional American specialty and seems to appear only around the fall holidays in certain parts of the country. My version is every bit as good as pumpkin pie, only not as well known. So here is a very simple, homey time-saving version using a food processor. It was inspired by the marshmallow-topped sweet potatoes served at my family's Thanksgiving dinners. I've put the same topping on this pie, and it's as good here as it is on all those casseroles!

➤ *Equipment Needed:* ★ 9-INCH PIE PLATE ★ PIE WEIGHTS ★ FOOD PROCESSOR WITH BLADE ★ ELECTRIC MIXER

❦ Crust:

1½ cups all-purpose flour

1 tablespoon sugar

8 tablespoons (1 stick) cold unsalted butter, cut into tablespoons

4 to 6 tablespoons ice water

❦ Filling:

4 tablespoons (½ stick) unsalted butter, softened

⅓ cup sugar

1½ cups mashed sweet potatoes, fresh or canned unsweetened, well drained

2 large eggs, at room temperature

½ cup milk

1 tablespoon pure vanilla extract

½ teaspoon ground cinnamon

¼ teaspoon ground nutmeg

⅛ teaspoon ground ginger

Pinch of salt

½ cup marshmallow cream, as accompaniment

1½ to 2 cups miniature marshmallows, for topping

Make the crust:

1. In the bowl of the food processor, pulse the flour and sugar together several times until combined. Add the butter, 1 tablespoon at a time, pulsing after each addition, until it resembles coarse crumbs. With the processor on, drizzle the ice water, 1 tablespoon at a time, down the feed tube and process until the dough forms a ball. Remove the dough from the bowl, flatten it into a disk, wrap in plastic wrap, and refrigerate for 1 hour.
2. Preheat the oven to 400 degrees F.
3. On a lightly floured surface, roll the dough out to fit the 9-inch pie plate with a 2-inch overhang. Transfer the dough into the pie plate, fold the overhang back over the dough to reinforce it, and trim and crimp the edges. Cover the shell with aluminum foil and line the foil with pie weights. Bake for 10 minutes. Remove the weights and foil, and bake the crust 5 minutes more. Remove to a wire rack to cool.
4. Lower the oven temperature to 350 degrees F.

Make the filling:

5. Put the butter and sugar in a bowl and cream together until fluffy, 4 to 5 minutes, using the electric mixer on medium speed. Add the mashed sweet potatoes, eggs, and milk, and beat until combined. Add the vanilla, spices, and salt, and blend well.
6. In a ceramic or glass cup heat the marshmallow cream, covered with plastic wrap, in a microwave oven on High for 15-second intervals until soft. Spread the cream over the prebaked crust.
7. Pour the filling into the prebaked crust and bake the pie for 45 minutes. Remove to a wire rack and immediately sprinkle the marshmallows over the top. Return the pie to the oven and bake about 15 minutes more, until the topping is golden brown and puffy, and a knife inserted in the center comes out clean. Remove the pie to the rack and let it cool for 30 minutes. The pie can be served warm or at room temperature.

Spiced Sweet Potato Pie with Nuts

≽ *Makes 8 servings* ≼

*T*his is definitely a grown-up version of sweet potato pie.

What I love about the holidays is all the baking activity and a houseful of friends and family. On Thanksgiving I like to serve both of my sweet potato pies: The marshmallow one goes to the kids' table; this one is reserved for the adults. If you want, remove some of the brandy from the filling and whip it into a little sweetened heavy cream. Garnish the pie with the whipped cream or serve it alongside.

≽ *Equipment Needed:* ★ 9-INCH PIE PLATE

❦ Crust:

1 cup all-purpose flour, sifted
½ teaspoon salt
6 tablespoons (¾ stick) cold unsalted butter
¾ cup finely chopped almonds, toasted
2 tablespoons ice water

❦ Filling:

1 cup mashed sweet potatoes, fresh or canned unsweetened, well drained
1 cup evaporated milk
1¼ cups firmly packed light brown sugar
3 large eggs, lightly beaten
¼ cup brandy
1 teaspoon pumpkin pie spice
½ teaspoon salt
½ cup chopped pecans

Make the crust:

1. In a bowl, whisk together the flour and salt. With a pastry cutter, cut in the butter until the mixture is coarsely textured with small, irregular flakes and bits the size of small peas. Stir in the almonds until combined. Sprinkle on the water, 1 tablespoon at a time, stirring with a fork until the dough just holds together. Gather the dough into a ball, flatten it into a disk, wrap it in plastic wrap, and refrigerate it for 1 hour.

142 ★ ★ ★ *Great American Desserts* ★ ★

2. On a lightly floured surface, roll out the dough into a ⅛-inch-thick round. Fit the dough into the pie pan, trim the edges, and crimp decoratively. Chill the shell in the freezer while making the filling.

3. Preheat the oven to 400 degrees F.

Make the filling:

4. In a large bowl, stir together the sweet potatoes, milk, and sugar until combined. Stir in the eggs, brandy, pie spice, salt, and pecans, and combine well.

5. Pour the filling into the chilled pie shell and bake for 20 minutes. Lower the oven temperature to 325 degrees F. and bake the pie 30 to 35 minutes more, or until the tip of a sharp knife inserted in the center comes out clean.

   Remove the pie from the oven to a wire rack and cool for 30 minutes. The pie may be served warm or at room temperature.

Chapter 6

Brownies and Bar Cookies

How did we ever live without brownies? This classic American bar cookie of chocolate, butter, sugar, flour, eggs, and sometimes—but not always—nuts has provided more pleasure and inspired more variations than almost any other cookie known to mankind. Should they be cakey or fudgy? Iced or plain? Nutted or not? Is more chocolate better, or more butter, or both? Is underbaking the key? Each brownie lover has his or her own opinion.

For something so loved, you'd think the origin of the first brownie would be perfectly documented. It isn't. One theory goes that brownies were born from a fire in the kitchen of a Boston hotel when the chef in the smoky confusion accidentally combined butter cookie batter with some melted chocolate. Another story goes that a woman in Maine forgot to add baking powder to her chocolate cake batter. What *is* sure is that the first recipe for brownies was printed in a Sears, Roebuck catalog back in 1897.

Just shy of one hundred years, the brownie is still one of America's favorites, and certainly one of mine. My flourless brownie variation (page 146), for example, is almost a fudge; my Chunky Brazil Nut Brownies combine (page 148) two kinds of chocolate with those marvelous rich nuts and, you guessed it, caramel. I've even added old-fashioned rolled oats to brownies for a very unusual treat!

Blondies, brownielike bar cookies without the chocolate, are no less delicious.

Despite what a brownie or blondie lover might tell you, there's more to bar cookies than just those two. Two that I make often—both very tart and absolutely great—are lemon bars and a great lemon-blueberry variation.

Debbi's Flourless Fudge Brownies

*Y*ou'll need a total of 22 ounces of chocolate for these brownies, which gives you some idea of how wonderfully rich they are! And, yes, they are flourless, so they won't rise the way other brownies do in the pan. These are dense and delicious—there's nothing cakelike about them—and as the recipe indicates, they must be made in advance, chilled, and then brought back almost to room temperature for you to experience their incredible flavor and texture. High-quality chocolate makes them even better.

➤ *Equipment Needed:* ★ 9-INCH SQUARE BAKING PAN ★ ELECTRIC MIXER

6 large eggs

18 ounces semisweet chocolate, chopped

16 tablespoons (2 sticks) unsalted butter, cut into tablespoons

1 teaspoon pure vanilla extract

▼ Glaze:

¼ cup heavy cream

4 ounces semisweet chocolate, chopped

24 pecan halves, toasted, for topping

1. Preheat the oven to 425 degrees F. Butter the baking pan, line it with aluminum foil, and butter the foil. Set the eggs in a bowl and cover them with hot tap water.

2. In the top of a double boiler set over barely simmering water, melt the chocolate with the butter, stirring until smooth. Stir in the vanilla. Transfer the mixture to a bowl and let it cool slightly on a rack.

3. Put the warm eggs in a large bowl and beat using the electric mixer on high speed until about triple in volume, about 5 minutes. Fold half of the beaten eggs into the chocolate mixture to lighten it. Gently fold in the remaining beaten eggs. Scrape the batter into the prepared pan and smooth the top.

4. Set the pan of batter in a larger baking pan. Pour hot water into the larger pan to come halfway up the sides of the brownie pan.

5. Bake the brownies on the middle rack of the oven for 10 minutes. Turn off the oven and let the brownies stand in the oven for 5 minutes. Remove the brownies from the water-bath to a wire rack and let stand while you make the glaze.

Make the glaze:

6. In a small ceramic or glass bowl covered with plastic wrap, heat the cream with the chocolate on High in a microwave oven for 30-second intervals, stirring after each interval, until smooth.

7. Pour the hot glaze evenly over the surface of the brownies. Spread it with a rubber spatula until smooth and let cool completely. When cool, cover the pan with plastic wrap and refrigerate until well chilled and firm, about 4 hours, or overnight.

8. To serve, cut into 12 squares and top each with pecans. Arrange the brownies on a serving plate. For the best flavor and texture, let the brownies stand at room temperature 20 to 30 minutes before serving.

Chunky Brazil Nut Brownies

➤ Makes 12 brownies ◄

*I*f flourless brownies are rich, these are fudgier and richer still, with Brazil nuts, white chocolate, cocoa, and caramel added. Incredibly delicious—a cross between candy and a brownie—these make a marvelous dessert and a very special hostess gift, too.

➤ *Equipment Needed:* ★ 8-INCH SQUARE BAKING PAN ★ ELECTRIC MIXER

12 tablespoons (1½ sticks) unsalted butter, melted

1 cup unsweetened cocoa powder

¾ cup sugar

½ cup firmly packed dark brown sugar

2 large eggs, at room temperature

1 teaspoon pure vanilla extract

¾ cup all-purpose flour

¼ teaspoon salt

1 cup semisweet chocolate chips

1 cup chopped white chocolate

1 cup skinned and chopped Brazil nuts, toasted (see Tip, page 149)

20 soft caramel squares (5 to 6 ounces)

1. Preheat the oven to 350 degrees F. Butter the baking pan, line it with aluminum foil, and butter the foil.

2. In a large bowl, whisk together the melted butter and cocoa powder until smooth. With an electric mixer on medium speed beat in the white and brown sugars until combined. Beat in the eggs and the vanilla until combined.

3. In a bowl, whisk together the flour and salt. Stir the flour mixture into the butter mixture. Add the chocolate chips, white chocolate pieces, and Brazil nuts. Do not overbeat. Spread the batter in the prepared baking pan and smooth the top.

4. In a ceramic or glass bowl covered with plastic wrap, melt the caramels with 2 tablespoons water on Medium in a microwave oven, stirring occasionally, for 2 to 3 minutes, or until melted. Drizzle the melted caramel over the batter in the pan and with the tip of a knife swirl it into the batter.

5. Bake the brownies for 25 to 30 minutes, or until the edges are set. (When tested the center will still be moist but should not be runny.) Remove the pan to a wire rack and cool completely in the pan.

6. To serve, cut the brownies into 2 by 2½-inch pieces and arrange on a serving plate.

➢ *Tip:* Brazil Nuts

Brazil nuts, the seeds of a tree that grows in the Amazon jungle, have extremely hard shells that are difficult to remove. To save yourself a lot of aggravation, buy the nuts shelled and skinned!

Chocolate Caramel Oat Brownies

> *Makes 18 bars*

*T*hree textures come into play with these one-of-a-kind brownies. Caramel and nuts in the middle make them chewy and crunchy, and a wonderful brown sugar–oatmeal dough makes them crumbly from bottom to top. My daughters love these with a big glass of cold milk. And so do I!

> *Equipment Needed:* ★ 9 BY 13-INCH BAKING PAN ★ FOOD PROCESSOR WITH METAL BLADE

1 1/2 cups all-purpose flour

1 1/2 cups old-fashioned rolled oats, toasted (see Tip: Types of Oats, page 227)

1 1/2 cups firmly packed dark brown sugar

1/2 teaspoon baking soda

1/4 teaspoon salt

12 tablespoons (1 1/2 sticks) cold unsalted butter, cut into tablespoons

12 ounces semisweet chocolate chips

2 cups chopped pecans, toasted

1/2 cup heavy cream

14 ounces caramel squares

1. Preheat the oven to 350 degrees F. Butter the baking pan, line it with aluminum foil, and butter the foil.
2. In the food processor, pulse the flour, oats, brown sugar, baking soda, and salt together just to combine. Add the butter, a few pieces at a time, and cut it into the dry ingredients by turning the machine on and off quickly. Process until the mixture is coarsely textured with small, irregular flakes and bits the size of small peas. (If combining by hand: In a bowl, whisk together the dry ingredients, then, with a pastry cutter, cut in the butter.)
3. Remove 2 cups of the crumb mixture and set aside. Press the remaining crumb mixture over the bottom of the baking pan. Sprinkle the chocolate chips and chopped pecans evenly over the crumb mixture. Set the pan aside.
4. In a heavy-bottomed, medium-size saucepan, bring the cream to a simmer over medium heat. Add the caramels, turn the heat to low, and melt them, stirring constantly, until smooth. Pour the caramel sauce over the chips and nuts in the baking pan. Sprinkle the reserved crumb mixture evenly over the top, pressing it down lightly with a metal spatula.

5. Bake the brownies for about 15 minutes, until the edges are golden brown. Remove the pan to a wire rack, and while the brownies are still warm, cut around the sides of the pan with a metal spatula to loosen the edges. Let the brownies cool on the rack to room temperature.

6. Cut the brownies into 2 by 3-inch pieces. Arrange on a serving plate, cover with plastic wrap, and refrigerate until well chilled, about 3 hours.

7. Let the brownies stand at room temperature about 15 minutes before serving.

Debbi's Blondies

➤ *Makes 18 pieces* ◄

I've made great blondies for years just adding pecans to the traditional butter, brown sugar, egg, and flour batter. I've discovered, though, that if you combine butterscotch sauce with some toasted pecans and swirl the mixture through the batter, you get the best blondies ever. I've used store-bought sauce because it makes these easy-to-make bar cookies even easier, especially for the kids. But if you're inspired to make your own, it will make these luscious squares even more special.

➤ *Equipment Needed:* ★ 9 BY 13-INCH BAKING PAN ★ ELECTRIC MIXER

16 tablespoons (2 sticks) unsalted butter, softened	1 teaspoon baking soda
1½ cups firmly packed light brown sugar	½ teaspoon salt
3 large eggs, at room temperature	½ cup store-bought butterscotch or caramel sauce
1 tablespoon pure vanilla extract	
2½ cups sifted all-purpose flour	½ cup chopped pecans, toasted

1. Preheat the oven to 325 degrees F. Butter the baking pan, line the pan with aluminum foil, and butter the foil.

2. Put the butter and sugar in a bowl and blend together just until smooth using the electric mixer on medium speed. Do not whip.

3. In a small bowl, stir together the eggs and vanilla. On low speed, blend the egg mixture into the butter mixture until combined. Scrape down the bowl.

4. In a bowl, whisk together the flour, baking soda, and salt. Add the flour mixture to the egg mixture and beat on low speed until just combined. Scrape the batter into the prepared pan.

5. In a ceramic or glass bowl, covered with plastic wrap, warm the butterscotch sauce in a microwave oven on High for 30-second intervals until liquid. (Or heat it in a saucepan over low heat.) Stir in the pecans. With a spoon, drizzle the sauce evenly over the top of the brownies. With the tip of a knife, swirl the sauce into the batter just below the surface.

6. Bake the blondies for 25 to 30 minutes, or until the top is a light golden brown and the center is still slightly soft. Be careful not to overbake because this will dry out the crumb. Cool the blondies in the pan on a wire rack for 30 minutes, then lift them out of the pan using the edges of the foil.

7. To serve, cut the blondies into 2 by 3-inch pieces and arrange on a serving plate.

Butterscotch Blondies

➢ Makes 18 pieces ◄

I admit that I can't resist the flavor of caramel! So here I've added a homemade caramel sauce to a traditional chocolate chip blondie and then topped it with pieces of butter toffee candy. The double dose of butterscotch makes these very sweet, a little crunchy, and absolutely delicious. More extravagant still is serving these squares with a scoop of vanilla ice cream on top.

➢ *Equipment Needed:* ★ 9 BY 13-INCH BAKING PAN ★ ELECTRIC MIXER

❦ Blondies:

12 tablespoons (1½ sticks) unsalted butter,
  softened
2¼ cups firmly packed light brown sugar
3 large eggs, at room temperature
1 teaspoon pure vanilla extract
2⅔ cups all-purpose flour
1 teaspoon baking soda
¼ teaspoon salt
12 ounces semisweet chocolate chips

❦ Topping:

1½ tablespoons unsalted butter
¼ cup milk
½ cup plus 2 tablespoons powdered sugar
⅓ cup firmly packed light brown sugar
¾ cup butter toffee pieces

1. Preheat the oven to 350 degrees F. Butter the baking pan, line the pan with aluminum foil, and butter the foil.

Make the blondies:

2. Put the butter and sugar in a bowl and blend together until smooth using the electric mixer on medium speed. Do not whip.

3. In a small bowl, stir together the eggs and vanilla. Add the egg mixture to the butter mixture and blend on low speed until combined. Scrape down the bowl.

4. In a bowl, whisk together the flour, baking soda, and salt. Add the flour mixture to the egg mixture and beat on low speed until just combined. Stir in the chocolate chips, then scrape the batter into the prepared pan.

5. Bake the blondies for 25 to 30 minutes, or until the center is no longer runny when tested with a wooden skewer. Remove the blondies to a wire rack to cool.

Make the topping:

6. In a small saucepan, combine the butter and milk over medium heat until the butter is melted. Add the powdered and brown sugars, and stir until melted. Increase the heat to

medium-high, bring the mixture just barely to a simmer, and simmer for 5 minutes, until the mixture begins to thicken. Remove the pan from the heat.

7. Poke holes in the top of the baked blondies with a wooden skewer, then pour the caramel topping over the cake. Sprinkle the butter toffee pieces over the topping and let cool to set.

8. To serve, cut the blondies into 2 by 3-inch pieces and place on a serving plate.

Peanut Butter Mississippi Mud Bars

➤ *Makes 12 bars* ◀

*B*elieve it or not, it *is* possible to improve upon the combination of peanut butter and chocolate in a bar cookie. Just drop a little white chocolate into the batter, add a marbleized chocolate icing, then top it all off with a scattering of toasted pecans! Your family and friends won't believe how incredibly easy these are to make. We always have a batch on hand during the Christmas holidays, but don't wait to make these until then. These are a must-bake bar year round.

➤ *Equipment Needed:* ★ 8-INCH OR 9-INCH SQUARE BAKING PAN
                              ★ ELECTRIC MIXER

8 tablespoons (1 stick) unsalted butter, softened

1 cup firmly packed light brown sugar

1/2 cup creamy peanut butter

1 large egg, at room temperature

1 tablespoon pure vanilla extract

1 cup all-purpose flour

1/2 teaspoon baking soda

1/4 teaspoon salt

8 ounces white chocolate, coarsely chopped and divided into two 4-ounce portions

8 ounces semisweet chocolate, coarsely chopped and divided into two 4-ounce portions

1 cup coarsely chopped pecans, toasted and divided into two 1/2-cup portions

1. Preheat the oven to 325 degrees F. Butter the baking pan, line it with aluminum foil, and butter the foil.

2. Put the butter and sugar in a large bowl and blend until smooth using the electric mixer on medium speed. Beat in the peanut butter until smooth.

3. Stir the egg and vanilla together in a bowl and add to the peanut butter mixture until combined.

4. In a small bowl, whisk together the flour, baking soda, and salt. Add to the butter mixture and combine well.

5. Stir in 1 portion each of the white and semisweet chocolates and combine. Add 1 portion of the pecans and mix until combined.

6. Spread the batter evenly in the prepared pan and bake for 30 to 35 minutes, or until the center is soft but no longer runny. Remove the pan from the oven and immediately sprinkle the remaining white and semisweet chocolates over the top. Cover the pan with aluminum foil and set aside to let the chocolates melt.

7. When melted, swirl the chocolates together with the tip of a sharp knife to make a marbleized effect. Sprinkle the remaining pecans over the top. Let the bars cool completely in the pan on a wire rack.

8. To serve, cut into 2-inch squares and arrange on a serving plate.

Peanut Butter, Fruit, and Nut Bars

➤ *Makes 18 bars* ⬅

I call these my "energy bars." They combine a chocolate crust, peanut butter, three different kinds of nuts, two different dried fruits, and coconut! These chewy bars are as pretty to look at as they are good to eat and are a definite change of pace when you want some quick perking up. Stash these in lunchboxes or backpacks, or just put them out after school for a fantastic treat.

➤ *Equipment Needed:* ★ 9 BY 13-INCH BAKING PAN ★ ELECTRIC MIXER

♦ Chocolate crust:

2½ ounces unsweetened chocolate, chopped

8 tablespoons (1 stick) unsalted butter, softened

1 cup sugar

2 large eggs, at room temperature

½ cup all-purpose flour

¼ teaspoon salt

1 teaspoon pure vanilla extract

¾ cup finely chopped pecans, toasted

♦ Topping:

¾ cup chunky peanut butter

½ cup firmly packed light brown sugar

4 large eggs, at room temperature, lightly beaten

1 cup semisweet chocolate chips

¾ cup finely chopped unsalted peanuts, toasted

½ cup finely chopped almonds, toasted

½ cup chopped dried apricots

⅓ cup chopped pitted dates

½ cup flaked sweetened coconut

1. Preheat the oven to 350 degrees F. Butter the baking pan lightly, line it with aluminum foil, and lightly butter the foil.

Make the chocolate crust:

2. In a ceramic or glass bowl covered with plastic wrap, heat the chocolate on High in a microwave oven for 30-second intervals, stirring after each interval, until smooth. Let cool slightly.

3. Put the butter and sugar in a bowl and cream together until fluffy, 4 to 5 minutes, using the electric mixer on medium speed. Add the eggs, melted chocolate, flour, salt, and vanilla, and beat until well combined. Stir in the pecans.

4. Press the mixture over the bottom of the prepared baking pan and bake for 15 minutes. Let cool on a wire rack while making the topping.

5. Lower the oven temperature to 325 degrees F.

Make the topping:

6. Put the peanut butter and brown sugar in a bowl and blend until smooth using the electric mixer on medium speed. Scrape down the bowl. Add the eggs and beat until well combined. Stir in the chocolate chips, peanuts, almonds, apricots, coconut, and dates and combine thoroughly.

7. Pour the topping over the baked crust, spreading it evenly, and bake for 30 to 35 minutes. Remove the pan to a wire rack to cool completely before lifting from the pan, using the edges of the foil.

8. To serve, cut into 2 by 3-inch bars and arrange on a serving plate.

Lemon-Lime Squares

*L*emon squares are a tried-and-true American favorite, and these have a special twist. Now they're in a league of their own. Fresh lime juice and a little grated lime peel make these especially tart and tangy. I like to serve these squares in the summer, with fresh strawberries and a bowl of powdered sugar for dipping. I don't think you'll have leftovers when you serve them, and that's just fine! Because of the delicate, flaky crust, these are best served the day you bake them.

➤ *Equipment Needed:* ★ 8-INCH BAKING PAN ★ PIE WEIGHTS
★ ELECTRIC MIXER

❦ Crust:

1 cup all-purpose flour

¼ cup sugar

6 tablespoons (¾ stick) cold unsalted butter, cut into small chunks

1 large egg yolk mixed with 1 tablespoon ice water

Additional ice water

❦ Filling:

3 large egg whites, at room temperature

¾ cup sugar

1½ teaspoons grated fresh lemon peel (from 1 medium lemon) (see Tip, page 159)

1½ teaspoons grated fresh lime peel (from 2 medium limes)

2 tablespoons all-purpose flour

½ teaspoon baking powder

¼ teaspoon salt

¼ cup fresh lemon juice

¼ cup fresh lime juice

Powdered sugar, for dusting

1. Butter the pan, line it with aluminum foil, and butter the foil.

Make the crust:

2. In a bowl, whisk together the flour and sugar. With a pastry cutter, cut in the butter until the mixture is coarsely textured with small, irregular flakes and bits the size of small peas. Stir in the egg yolk–water mixture with a fork until combined, adding more ice water by the tablespoon until the dough can be gathered into a ball. Press the dough evenly over the bottom of the baking pan and prick it with a fork. Freeze the dough for 20 minutes.

3. Preheat the oven to 400 degrees F.

4. Cover the dough with a piece of aluminum foil, weight it down with pie weights, and bake the crust for 15 minutes. Lower the oven temperature to 375 degrees F. Remove the pie weights and foil, and bake 10 minutes more. Cool the crust on a wire rack while making the filling.

Make the filling:

5. Put the egg whites, sugar, and lemon and lime peels in a bowl and beat until frothy using the electric mixer on medium speed.

6. In a small bowl, whisk together the flour, baking powder, and salt.

7. Add the flour mixture to the egg white mixture and fold it in well. Fold in the lemon and lime juices. Pour the filling over the prebaked crust.

8. Bake for 20 minutes, or until the top is golden brown and firm when gently pressed with your finger. Remove the pan to a wire rack to cool.

9. To serve, cut into 2-inch squares using a sharp knife sprayed with nonstick cooking spray. Dust the squares lightly with powdered sugar and arrange on a serving plate.

➤ *Tip:* GRATING CITRUS FRUITS

I like to use a zester for grating citrus fruits. Small, easy-to-manage, handled utensils, zesters are available at any good kitchenware store.

Remember, you want only the colored skin of the fruit. Avoid the white skin beneath it, called the pith, which is bitter and will affect the taste of your cookies or cake if added.

Juice the fruits that you've zested, then freeze the juice, always a useful ingredient to have on hand.

Lemon-Berry Bars

⋟ *Makes 18 pieces* ⋞

*A*n unusual creamy filling with plenty of lemon flavor sets these lemon bars apart from all others I've ever tasted. You can serve the blueberry topping chilled, as suggested below, but it's also very special heated and then spooned over the chilled bars.

⋟ *Equipment Needed:* ★ 9 BY 13-INCH BAKING PAN ★ PIE WEIGHTS ★ ELECTRIC MIXER

⋓ Crust:

1½ cups all-purpose flour

3 tablespoons sugar

¼ teaspoon salt

2 teaspoons grated fresh lemon peel (from 1 lemon)

(see Tip: Grating Citrus Fruits, page 159)

8 tablespoons (1 stick) cold unsalted butter, cut into pieces

3 to 4 tablespoons ice water

⋓ Filling:

16 ounces cream cheese, softened

½ cup sugar

3 large eggs, at room temperature

¼ cup fresh lemon juice

2 teaspoons pure lemon extract

⋓ Blueberry topping:

1 cup sugar

¼ cup cornstarch

32 ounces frozen unsweetened blueberries, thawed and drained, juices reserved

1. Butter the baking pan, line it with aluminum foil, and butter the foil.

Make the crust:

2. In a bowl, whisk together the flour, sugar, salt, and lemon peel. With a pastry cutter, cut in the butter until the mixture is coarsely textured with small, irregular flakes and bits the size of small peas.

3. Add the ice water, 1 tablespoon at a time, mixing with a fork until the dough can be gathered into a ball. Press the dough evenly over the bottom of the baking pan, making sure it reaches into the corners, and prick it all over with a fork. Freeze the dough for 20 minutes.

4. Preheat the oven to 400 degrees F.

5. Cover the dough with aluminum foil, line the foil with pie weights, and bake the crust for 15 minutes. Lower the oven temperature to 375 degrees F. Remove the pie weights and foil, and bake the crust 10 minutes more. Remove the crust to a wire rack to cool while you prepare the filling. Lower the oven temperature to 325 degrees F.

Make the filling:

6. Put the cream cheese and sugar in a bowl and cream until smooth using the electric mixer on medium speed. Scrape down the bowl. Add the eggs, 1 at a time, beating for 20 seconds after each addition. Scrape down the bowl again. Beat in the lemon juice and lemon extract. Combine the filling completely using a rubber spatula, then scrape it evenly over the cooled crust.

7. Bake for 30 minutes. Turn off the oven and let the pan stand in the oven another 15 to 20 minutes. The top will be lightly golden, and the center will still be slightly jiggly when the pan is moved but should not be runny. Remove the pan to a wire rack to cool to room temperature. When cool, cover the pan with foil and refrigerate it for at least 2 hours.

Make the topping:

8. In a heavy, medium-size saucepan, whisk together the sugar and cornstarch. Slowly pour in the reserved blueberry juice, whisking until smooth. Over medium-high heat, cook the mixture, stirring constantly, until the sauce reaches a boil. Immediately lower the heat to maintain a simmer and continue cooking until the mixture thickens and turns glossy, 2 to 3 minutes. Stir in the blueberries and bring the mixture back to a simmer, stirring occasionally. Remove the pan from the heat, transfer the topping to a bowl, and cool on a rack.

9. With a sharp knife, cut the cold pastry and filling into bars 2 by 3 inches each and arrange them on a serving plate. To serve, top each bar with a spoonful of the blueberries. Pass the remaining topping separately.

Chapter 7

Other American Cookies

Where to begin?

There are so many different types of cookies to choose from: drop cookies, rolled cookies, refrigerator cookies, molded cookies, sandwich cookies. Some are elegant, some are plain, some are cookie-jar simple, some are decorated.

Let's start with shortbread cookies, a Scottish import that Americans have taken to heart. Simple and buttery rich, they are infinitely adaptable. I love nut shortbread (Pecan Butter Cookies are on page 173) and, of course, chocolate, so I've combined two shortbread doughs in one cookie for a marvelous fancy black-and-white swirl.

As for my cookie-jar cookie, you can't get more homegrown than oatmeal raisin, with a variation that's chunky with pieces of chocolate. If you love chewy, moist oatmeal cookies the way I do, you'll want to make two batches of these at a time! And let your children help because these are easy to make.

If you're looking for a special occasion cookie, you'll want to try Lemon Wedding Cookies (page 169) and Chocolate Wedding Cookies with nuts (page 171). Both are dredged in powdered sugar for a very special look. And whatever you do, please don't pass up Caramel Macadamia Butter Cookies on page 175. Made in an utterly unique way, these cookies with a caramel topping are the most elegant of all.

Two refrigerator cookies end this chapter on a particularly sweet note. To save some time for future cookie baking, why not always have a log or two of the dough in your freezer to bake when you have the chance?

The Dutch settlers are credited with having made the cookie popular in this country as a snack. I must say I don't think of cookies as a snack. I think of them as a way of life!

Debbi's Shortbread

*I*t's easy to understand why shortbread has remained as popular as it has since it came to these shores from Scotland so long ago. It's buttery and crumbly and sweet—simple to prepare but incredibly delicious. Some shortbread lovers don't add any flavoring at all to this classic cookie, but I've added a touch of almond extract.

The pieces of shortbread can be cut out as daintily as you like. I always use an assortment of my favorite cookie cutters, and I get a lot of help from my daughters. That's the fun part—that, and those first few bites! If you want to make these a little fancier as I often do, dip the cooled cookies in melted chocolate.

For best results, bake these cookies until golden just around the edges.

≽ *Equipment Needed:*   ★   2 COOKIE SHEETS   ★   BAKING PARCHMENT
★   2-INCH COOKIE CUTTERS

2 cups all-purpose flour	16 tablespoons (2 sticks) cold unsalted butter,
½ cup sugar	cut into chunks
Pinch of salt	1 teaspoon pure almond extract

1. In a bowl, whisk together the flour, sugar, and salt.
2. With a pastry cutter, cut the butter into the dry ingredients until it is evenly distributed and the size of small crumbs. Stir in the almond extract and mix the dough, shaping it with your hands, until it comes together to form a ball that is still slightly moist.
3. Transfer the dough to a lightly floured work surface and roll it out until it's ⅜ inch thick. Dip your favorite cookie cutter into flour and cut out shapes, transferring them to a cookie sheet and reflouring the cutter as needed. Cover the cookies with plastic wrap and chill them on the cookie sheet for 30 to 45 minutes.
4. While the cookies chill, preheat the oven to 325 degrees F. Line another cookie sheet with baking parchment and arrange the cookies on it, leaving about 1 inch between.
5. Bake the cookies for 18 to 20 minutes, or until they are golden around the edges. Remove the cookies with a spatula to wire racks to cool. Store in airtight tins in layers separated by

baking parchment or wax paper, or stack them in reclosable plastic bags. The cookies can also be frozen, wrapped first in plastic wrap and then in aluminum foil.

Chocolate Swirled Shortbread

➢ *Makes 2 dozen cookies* ◁

*O*nce, while I was about to bake a batch of plain shortbread cookies with my daughters, Ashley asked if we could add chocolate. So, thanks to Ashley, here is the black-and-white swirled variation—the best of all possible shortbread worlds!

A tin of these cookies makes a wonderful gift during the holidays. And for friends who like the taste of mocha, an optional spoonful or two of instant coffee crystals can be added.

I like to serve these in the afternoon with coffee; the flavors of chocolate and coffee seem just made for each other. They're good with a mug of hot cocoa, too.

➢*Equipment Needed:* ★ COOKIE SHEET ★ BAKING PARCHMENT
★ ELECTRIC MIXER

❦ Vanilla shortbread:

2 cups all-purpose flour

$^1/_2$ cup sugar

Pinch of salt

16 tablespoons (2 sticks) cold unsalted butter, cut into chunks

1 teaspoon pure vanilla extract

❦ Chocolate shortbread:

4 ounces semisweet chocolate, chopped

$1^1/_2$ cups all-purpose flour

$^1/_2$ cup powdered sugar

2 tablespoons unsweetened cocoa powder

$^1/_8$ teaspoon salt

12 tablespoons ($1^1/_2$ sticks) unsalted butter, softened

1 teaspoon pure vanilla extract combined with 2 tablespoons instant coffee crystals (optional)

1. Preheat the oven to 325 degrees F. Line a cookie sheet with baking parchment.

Make the vanilla shortbread:

2. In a large bowl, whisk together the flour, sugar, and salt. With a pastry cutter, cut the butter into the dry ingredients until it is evenly distributed and the size of small crumbs. Stir in the vanilla and mix the dough, shaping it with your hands until it comes together to form a ball.

3. Transfer the dough to a lightly floured work surface and roll it out until ¼ inch thick. Cover with plastic wrap and set aside.

Make the chocolate shortbread:

4. In a ceramic or glass bowl covered with plastic wrap, heat the chocolate in a microwave oven on High for 30-second intervals, stirring after each interval, until smooth. Let cool to lukewarm.

5. In a bowl, whisk together the flour, sugar, cocoa, and salt.

6. Put the butter in a bowl and whip until light and fluffy using the electric mixer on medium speed. Add the melted chocolate and beat until smooth. Beat in the vanilla and instant coffee, if using. Add the dry ingredients and combine until a dough forms. Gather the dough into a disk and flatten it slightly. On a lightly floured surface, roll it out until ¼ inch thick. (Should the dough be too soft to roll, wrap it in plastic wrap and chill until firm.)

7. Place the chocolate dough on top of the plain shortbread dough and with your hands gently but firmly roll the doughs into a log. Wrap the log in plastic wrap and chill for about 1 hour, or until firm.

8. With a sharp knife, cut the chilled dough into slices about ½ inch thick and arrange them on the prepared cookie sheet, leaving 1 inch between.

9. Bake the cookies for about 20 minutes, or until golden around the edges. Remove the cookies with a spatula to wire racks to cool. Store in any sealed container, such as a tin or jar. The cookies can also be frozen, wrapped first in plastic wrap and then in aluminum foil.

Debbi's Oatmeal Raisin Cookies

➤ Makes 3½ dozen ◄

I like my oatmeal cookies soft and chewy, and these fill that bill to a tee. If you like yours a little crisper, bake these a minute or two longer. These cookies disappear as fast as I can make them. They're great in lunchboxes, for snacks, for dessert, for tea. Come to think of it, these are good anytime at all.

➤ Equipment Needed: ★ COOKIE SHEETS ★ ELECTRIC MIXER

2¼ cups all-purpose flour

½ cup quick oats (not instant, see Tip: Types of Oats, page 227)

¾ teaspoon baking soda

½ teaspoon salt

1½ cups firmly packed dark brown sugar

16 tablespoons (2 sticks) unsalted butter at room temperature, cut into tablespoons

2 large eggs, at room temperature

1 tablespoon pure vanilla extract

1½ cups raisins

1. In a large bowl, whisk together the flour, oats, baking soda, and salt.
2. Put the sugar in a bowl and beat for 2 minutes until fluffy using the electric mixer on medium speed. Add the butter, several pieces at a time, and beat until combined.
3. In a small bowl, lightly combine the eggs and vanilla.
4. Add the egg mixture to the butter mixture and beat until smooth using the mixer on low speed. Scrape down the bowl with a rubber spatula. Add the dry ingredients and beat until just combined—a light dusting of flour should still be visible in the dough. Mix in the raisins until evenly distributed. Scrape down the bowl again. Chill the dough for about 1 hour, or until firm.
5. Preheat the oven to 300 degrees F.
6. Drop the chilled dough by rounded teaspoons onto ungreased cookie sheets, leaving 2 inches in between, and bake for 22 to 23 minutes. When done, the cookies should still be slightly soft and the edges light golden in color. Remove the cookies with a spatula to a wire rack to cool. Store in layers separated by pieces of wax paper in airtight containers.

Chocolate Chunk Oatmeal Cookies

⇒ *Makes about 3½ dozen* ⇐

*T*hese oatmeal cookies are still soft and chewy—the only way I like them—but for a definite change of pace I added lots of chocolate chunks. And they can be made with even more chocolate flavor if you use a little crème de cacao—chocolate-flavored liqueur. Bake these, then watch them disappear; they're irresistible to children and grown-ups alike.

⇒ *Equipment Needed:* ★ COOKIE SHEET ★ ELECTRIC MIXER

2½ cups all-purpose flour

½ cup quick oats (not *instant*, see *Tip: Types of Oats*, page 227)

½ teaspoon baking soda

½ teaspoon salt

1 cup firmly packed light brown sugar

½ cup white sugar

16 tablespoons (2 sticks) unsalted butter at room temperature, cut into tablespoons

2 large eggs, at room temperature

1 tablespoon pure vanilla extract

1 tablespoon crème de cacao (optional)

16 ounces semisweet chocolate, cut into small chunks

1. In a large bowl, whisk together the flour, oats, baking soda, and salt.
2. Put the sugars in a large bowl and beat using an electric mixer on medium speed for 2 or 3 minutes until fluffy. Beat in the butter, several pieces at a time, until combined.
3. In a small bowl, whisk together the eggs, vanilla, and crème de cacao, if using.
4. Beat the egg mixture into the butter mixture until smooth using the mixer at low speed. Scrape down the bowl with a rubber spatula. Beat in the dry ingredients until just combined—a light dusting of flour should be visible in the dough. Add the chocolate chunks and mix until evenly distributed. Scrape down the bowl again. Refrigerate the dough for about 1 hour, or until firm.

5. Preheat the oven to 300 degrees F.

6. Drop the chilled dough by rounded tablespoons onto ungreased cookie sheets, leaving about 2 inches in between, and bake for 22 to 23 minutes. When done, the cookies should still be slightly soft and the edges light golden in color. Immediately remove the cookies with a spatula to a wire rack to cool. Store in layers separated by pieces of wax paper in an airtight container.

Lemon Wedding Cookies

Makes about 4 dozen

*J*ust the name wedding cookie suggests something special, and these are! They have the loveliest lemon flavor, and with ground almonds in both the dough and also around the outside of each cookie—my special touch—these are especially crumbly and nutty. Elegant with their powdery sugar cover, these are truly special occasion cookies.

Equipment Needed: ★ COOKIE SHEETS ★ ELECTRIC MIXER

18 tablespoons (2 sticks plus 2 table-
    spoons) unsalted butter, softened
¾ cup powdered sugar, plus 2 cups for
    dredging the cookies
1 tablespoon pure vanilla extract
¾ teaspoon pure lemon extract
3 tablespoons buttermilk
1¾ cups all-purpose flour
1½ cups finely ground toasted blanched
    almonds, plus 1 cup finely ground
    toasted almonds
2 teaspoons grated fresh lemon peel (see
    Tip: Grating Citrus Fruits, page 159)
⅛ teaspoon salt

1. Put the butter and sugar in a large bowl and cream together until fluffy, 4 to 5 minutes, using an electric mixer on medium speed. Add the vanilla and lemon extracts, and combine well. Beat in the buttermilk and scrape down the bowl.
2. In another bowl, combine the flour, 1½ cups of almonds, lemon peel, and salt.
3. Add the dry ingredients to the butter mixture and beat using the mixer on low speed. Scrape down the bowl. Refrigerate the dough for 1 hour, or until firm.
4. Preheat the oven to 325 degrees F.
5. Scoop the dough by level tablespoons and form each piece into a ball. Roll the balls in the remaining ground almonds. Place the balls 2 inches apart on cookie sheets.
6. Bake the cookies for 18 to 20 minutes, or until the edges just begin to turn golden. Remove the cookies with a spatula to a wire rack to cool to room temperature.
7. Dredge the cookies, a few at a time, in the powdered sugar and shake off the excess. Store in layers separated by pieces of wax paper in an airtight container.

Chocolate Wedding Cookies

*I*f the combination of toasted hazelnuts and chocolate is one of your favorites, this is the cookie for you. These wedding cookies are dark and rich, with a glossy two-chocolate glaze and nuts on top. These are definitely cookies worthy of a special occasion but I'd have them any day.

➤ *Equipment Needed:* ★ COOKIE SHEETS ★ ELECTRIC MIXER
★ FOOD PROCESSOR WITH METAL BLADE

12 tablespoons (1½ sticks) unsalted butter, softened

¾ cup firmly packed light brown sugar

4 ounces semisweet chocolate, melted

1 tablespoon pure vanilla extract

3 tablespoons buttermilk

1½ cups skinned, toasted hazelnuts (see Tip, page 172)

¼ cup white sugar

1½ cups all-purpose flour

½ teaspoon salt

3 ounces semisweet chocolate, chopped

❦ Chocolate glaze:

6 ounces milk chocolate, coarsely chopped

6 ounces semisweet chocolate, coarsely chopped

¼ cup heavy cream

1 generous cup skinned, toasted hazelnuts, chopped, for dipping

1. Put the butter and brown sugar in a bowl and cream together until fluffy, 4 to 5 minutes, using the electric mixer on medium speed. Add the melted chocolate and vanilla and beat on low speed until well blended. Beat in the buttermilk until smooth.

2. In the food processor, process the 1½ cups hazelnuts with the white sugar until finely ground. In a bowl, combine the nut mixture, flour, and salt.

3. Add the nut-flour mixture to the chocolate mixture and beat until just combined. Stir in the chopped chocolate. Refrigerate the dough for about 1 hour, or until firm.

4. Preheat the oven to 325 degrees F.

5. Scoop the dough by level tablespoons and form each piece into a ball. Place the balls 2 inches apart on cookie sheets.

6. Bake for 18 to 20 minutes. The tops will still be slightly soft when pressed. Immediately remove the cookies with a spatula to a wire rack to cool.

Make the chocolate glaze:

7. In a ceramic or glass bowl covered with plastic wrap, heat both chocolates with the cream on High in a microwave oven for 30-second intervals, stirring after each interval, until smooth. Cool slightly.

Dip the cookies:

8. Dip the top of each cookie into the glaze, letting the excess drip off, then dip into the chopped hazelnuts. Transfer the dipped cookies to a cookie sheet and chill them for 1 hour, or until the glaze is set. Store the cookies in layers separated by wax paper in an air-tight container.

➤ *Tip:* To Skin Hazelnuts

To skin hazelnuts, toast them on a cookie sheet in a preheated 350-degree oven for 10 minutes. Transfer the hazelnuts to a clean kitchen towel and rub them together to remove their loosened skins. (Not every last bit of skin will come off, but most of it should.)

Pecan Butter Cookies

*T*hese are wonderfully buttery nut cookies, similar to shortbread. I like them almost as much unglazed as I do glazed. Use your favorite cutters to shape them. We chose a heart shape, but stars are pretty, too. During warm weather months you'll want to remember to store these in a cool place.

➤ *Equipment Needed:* ★ COOKIE SHEETS ★ BLENDER OR FOOD PROCESSOR ★ ELECTRIC MIXER ★ 3-INCH COOKIE CUTTER

½ cup pecan pieces, toasted

½ cup sugar

8 tablespoons (1 stick) unsalted butter, softened

1 teaspoon pure vanilla extract

1 teaspoon grated fresh orange peel (see Tip: Grating Citrus Fruits, page 159)

1 large egg yolk, at room temperature

1¼ cups all-purpose flour

¾ teaspoon baking powder

¼ teaspoon salt

❦ Chocolate glaze:

1½ cups heavy cream

16 ounces semisweet chocolate, chopped into small pieces

1. In the blender or food processor, pulse the pecans with the sugar until the nuts are finely ground.
2. Put the butter and pecan-sugar mixture in a large bowl and cream together until fluffy using the electric mixer on medium speed. Add the vanilla, peel, and egg yolk and beat on low speed until combined. Scrape down the bowl.
3. In another bowl, whisk together the flour, baking powder, and salt.

4. Add the dry ingredients to the butter mixture and beat on low speed until combined. Scrape down the bowl. Gather the dough into a ball, flatten it into a disk, and wrap it in plastic wrap. Refrigerate for 1 hour, or until firm.

5. Preheat the oven to 325 degrees F.

6. On a lightly floured surface, roll the dough out until ⅛ inch thick. Cut out cookies using a 3-inch cookie cutter. Place them on a cookie sheet about 1 inch apart. Gather up the scraps, reroll the dough, and cut out cookies in the same manner.

7. Bake the cookies for 6 to 8 minutes, or until they just begin to turn golden around the edges. Remove the cookies with a spatula to a wire rack to cool.

Make the chocolate glaze:

8. In a medium-size ceramic or glass bowl covered with plastic wrap, heat the cream with the chocolate in a microwave oven on High for 30-second intervals, stirring after each interval, until smooth. Let cool for about 5 minutes. (Or, make the glaze in a heavy, medium-size saucepan over medium heat, bring the cream to a simmer. While it is heating, put the

chocolate in a bowl. Pour the hot cream over the chocolate and let sit for 2 minutes, then stir until smooth.)

9. Dip each cooled cookie halfway into the chocolate glaze, letting the excess drip off. Dry the glazed cookies on wax paper, then store in layers separated by wax paper in an airtight container.

Caramel Macadamia Butter Cookies

➤ *Makes 16 (2-inch) cookies* ◄

*T*hese butter cookies are almost confections, with their candylike topping of chocolate and nuts and caramel. Elegant to serve, beautiful to look at, and delicious to eat, they are also fun to make. Don't be too eager to remove the baked cookies from their cutters—an unusual piece of advice when it comes to baking! You leave the cookies in their molds as a way of keeping the toppings in place.

If you need to borrow some extra cookie cutters from friends, return them with at least one of these cookies still inside. You'll always have volunteers after that!

➤ *Equipment Needed:* ★ COOKIE SHEET ★ ELECTRIC MIXER ★ SIXTEEN 2-INCH ROUND METAL COOKIE CUTTERS

8 tablespoons (1 stick) unsalted butter, softened	1¼ cups all-purpose flour
½ cup sugar	¾ teaspoon baking soda
1 large egg yolk, at room temperature	¼ teaspoon salt
1 teaspoon pure vanilla extract	

❦ Caramel:

4 tablespoons (½ stick) unsalted butter, softened	1½ cups sugar
½ cup heavy cream, at room temperature	⅓ cup water
	1 teaspoon fresh lemon juice

♥ Chocolate glaze:

4 ounces milk chocolate, cut into small
    pieces
2 ounces semisweet chocolate, cut into
    small pieces
¼ cup heavy cream

1½ cups coarsely chopped toasted
    macadamia nuts, for sprinkling

1. Put the butter and sugar in a bowl and
   cream together using the electric mixer
   on medium speed. Add the egg yolk
   and vanilla and beat on low speed until
   combined. Scrape down the bowl.
2. In another bowl, whisk together the
   flour, baking soda, and salt.
3. Add the dry ingredients to the butter
   mixture and beat on low speed until combined. Scrape down the bowl. Gather the
   dough into a ball, flatten it into a disk, and wrap it in plastic wrap. Refrigerate the dough
   for 1 hour, or until firm. While the dough chills, make both the caramel and the
   chocolate glaze.

Make the caramel:

4. In a small ceramic or glass bowl covered with plastic wrap, heat the butter with the cream
   on High in a microwave oven for 45 seconds, or until the mixture is warm.
5. In a heavy, medium-size saucepan over medium heat, combine the sugar, water, and lemon
   juice, stirring constantly until the sugar dissolves. With a pastry brush dipped in cold
   water, brush down the sides of the pan to remove any sugar crystals. Increase the heat to
   medium-high and cook, swirling the pan occasionally, until the mixture turns light amber.
   Quickly remove the pan from the heat and slowly pour in the heated cream mixture. Be
   careful—the mixture will boil rapidly. Return the pan to medium heat and stir the mixture
   with a wooden spoon until smooth. Lower the heat to a simmer and cook the caramel
   until it thickens and lightly coats the spoon, 3 or 4 minutes. Remove the pan from the
   heat and with a rubber spatula scrape the caramel into a bowl. Cover and keep warm.

Make the chocolate glaze:

6. In a double boiler set over barely simmering water, combine the milk chocolate and semi-sweet chocolate with the cream and melt, stirring, until smooth. Keep the glaze warm.

7. Preheat the oven to 325 degrees F. Lightly coat the insides of the cookie cutters with non-stick vegetable spray.

8. On a lightly floured surface, roll out the dough until ⅛ inch thick. With the prepared cookie cutters, cut out shapes, leaving the dough inside each cutter. Place the cutters on a cookie sheet and bake until golden, 5 or 6 minutes. Transfer the cookies, still in the cutters, to a wire rack to cool.

Assemble the cookies:

9. Transfer the cookies in the cutters to a foil-lined cookie sheet. Drizzle 1 teaspoon of the chocolate glaze over each cookie in its mold, sprinkle with 1 tablespoon of chopped macadamia nuts, and top with 1 tablespoon of caramel. Transfer the sheet to the refrigerator and chill the cookies until set, about 1 hour.

10. To serve, remove the cookies from the cutters with a small, sharp knife, carefully running the blade around the inside edge of each mold. Arrange the cookies on a serving plate.

Debbi's Chewy Toffee Cookies

➤ *Makes about 3 dozen* ◄

I love candy in a cookie, and these have lots of chocolate-covered toffee bits throughout. If you're feeling fancy, you can pipe or drizzle these with a simple sugar glaze, but you don't have to—these "logs" are delicious just the way they are.

➤ *Equipment Needed:* ★ COOKIE SHEET   ★ BAKING PARCHMENT
★ ELECTRIC MIXER

½ cup firmly packed light brown sugar

¼ cup white sugar

8 tablespoons (1 stick) unsalted butter, cut
   into tablespoons and softened

¼ cup vegetable oil

3 large eggs, lightly beaten

1 tablespoon pure vanilla extract

3 cups all-purpose flour

1½ teaspoons baking powder

¼ teaspoon salt

1½ cups chocolate-covered toffee bits

1 cup pecan pieces, toasted

❦ Glaze (optional):

3 teaspoons milk
½ cup powdered sugar

1. Line a cookie sheet with baking parchment.
2. Put the brown and white sugars in a bowl and beat until fluffy using the electric mixer on
   medium speed. Add the butter and beat until combined. Add the oil and beat until combined. Beat in the eggs and vanilla. Scrape down the bowl.

3. In a bowl, whisk together the flour, baking powder, and salt.
4. Add the flour mixture to the butter mixture and beat on low speed until just combined. Add the toffee bits and pecans and stir until combined. Scrape down the bowl. Refrigerate the dough for at least 1 hour, or until firm.
5. Preheat the oven to 325 degrees F.
6. Gather the dough into a ball and cut it into 4 equal pieces. Shape each piece into a log 1½ by 8 inches. Put the logs on the prepared baking sheet, leaving 2 inches in between.
7. Bake the logs for 20 to 25 minutes. The tops will crack and a toothpick inserted in the center will come out clean, but the logs will still feel soft to the touch. Do not overbake. Transfer to a wire rack for 15 minutes, then cut into 1-inch pieces.

Make the (optional) glaze, if using:

8. In a small bowl, whisk the milk into the powdered sugar until smooth. Drizzle the glaze from the tines of a fork over the cookies. Store the cookies in layers separated by sheets of wax paper in an airtight container.

➤ *Tip:* HAVING COOKIE-DOUGH LOGS ON HAND

If you'd like to have cookies on hand, simply freeze the unbaked logs of dough, well sealed in plastic wrap and foil. Then it's just a matter of thawing the logs in the refrigerator overnight, baking, and slicing the cookies the next day.

Debbi's Nutty Mocha Cookies

⇒ *Makes about 3 dozen* ⇐

*C*risp on the outside but soft and moist within—my favorite combination of textures for a cookie!—these logs make a wonderful present. Lots of chocolate goes into this cookie dough, and the mocha accent is subtle—making these kid-friendly, too.

Like Chewy Toffee Cookies (page 177), the log-shaped dough can be frozen. In fact, I like to serve these with Chewy Toffee Cookies—they look especially pretty together.

⇒ *Equipment Needed:* ★ COOKIE SHEETS ★ BAKING PARCHMENT ★ ELECTRIC MIXER

8 tablespoons (1 stick) unsalted butter	2 tablespoons coffee liqueur
½ cup unsweetened cocoa powder	2½ cups all-purpose flour
3 large eggs, at room temperature, lightly beaten	1½ teaspoons baking powder
	¼ teaspoon salt
¾ cup white sugar	6 ounces white chocolate, coarsely chopped
½ cup firmly packed light brown sugar	6 ounces semisweet chocolate, coarsely chopped
1 tablespoon pure vanilla extract	1 cup coarsely chopped pecans, toasted

1. Line the cookie sheet with the baking parchment.
2. In a ceramic or glass bowl covered with plastic wrap, heat the butter in a microwave oven on High for 30-second intervals until melted. Whisk in the cocoa until smooth.
3. Put the eggs and white and brown sugars in a bowl and beat until fluffy, 4 to 5 minutes, using the electric mixer on medium speed. Scrape down the bowl. Add the butter mixture and beat until smooth. Add the vanilla and coffee liqueur, and beat until smooth. Scrape down the bowl.
4. In a bowl, whisk together the flour, baking powder, and salt.
5. Add the flour mixture to the butter mixture and beat on low speed until just combined. Stir in the white and semisweet chocolates and pecans until combined. Scrape down the bowl. Refrigerate the dough for at least 1 hour, or until firm.

6. Preheat the oven to 325 degrees F.

7. Gather the dough into a ball. Cut it into 4 equal pieces and shape each piece into a log 1½ by 8 inches. Put the logs on the prepared cookie sheet, leaving 2 inches in between.

8. Bake the logs for 25 to 30 minutes. The tops will crack, and a toothpick inserted in the center will come out clean, but the logs will still feel soft to the touch. Transfer the logs to a cutting board, cool for 15 minutes, then cut into 1-inch slices. Store the cookies in layers separated by wax paper in an airtight container.

9. If desired, drizzle the cookies with the glaze on page 178. Let dry before serving.

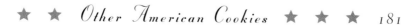

Chapter 8

Special Occasion Desserts

THE TEN SPECIAL OCCASION desserts that follow are as varied a grouping as any in this book! From simple poached pears to two of my favorite candies, with four chocolate desserts in between, there's a lot of temptation to ponder when planning your next celebration. Whether you're hosting an anniversary dinner, a family reunion, or a graduation gala, there's a dessert here to fit all tastes.

You'll find some surprises, too. Baked apples, a simple early-American dessert if there ever was one, has never been more elegant: Here they're poached, then filled and baked in a buttery crust.

Now let's move on to chocolate. From my own truffle cake (one of the easiest recipes in this book) to a *triple* truffle cake, stacked three layers high and thick with icing, to mousse pies, you have your pick of intense chocolate desserts.

Debbi's Poached Pears

➤ *Makes 6 servings* ◄

*T*he simplest way to poach pears is in sugar syrup, which undoubtedly many early Americans did as a way of using pears before they went bad. The modern dessert-maker has lots of other choices, including wine and liqueurs, but this recipe uses cran-raspberry juice for a change of pace. And I've added fresh citrus juice, which imparts a zesty flavor of its own.

These pears are a lower-calorie alternative to cake or pie, and make an elegant, simple, old-fashioned dessert. Mint leaves always add that special something when you're serving these at a special occasion, as would a few fresh raspberries to garnish the plate.

➤ *Equipment Needed:* ★ MELON BALLER

6 slightly underripe Bartlett pears

▼ Poaching liquid:

4 cups cran-raspberry juice
1 lemon, juiced and fruit quartered

1 orange, juiced and fruit quartered
1 cup sugar

▼ Garnish:

Mint leaves

Fresh raspberries (optional)

Make the poaching liquid:

1. In a 4-quart saucepan, combine the cran-raspberry juice, lemon and orange juices, cut-up fruits, and sugar, and bring to a simmer, stirring occasionally, to dissolve the sugar.
2. Meanwhile, peel each pear and with the melon baller scoop out the core from the bottom, extending about halfway into the fruit. Leave the stem end intact. Cut a slice off the bottom of each pear so that it stands upright.
3. Carefully add the pears to the simmering poaching liquid in the pan, standing them upright. If necessary, add water to the pan to come about three-quarters of the way up the

sides of the pears. Cover and simmer over low heat about 20 minutes, until just tender. Do not overcook. With a slotted spoon, remove the pears to a plate to cool.

4. Reduce the poaching liquid over high heat to 1 cup. Remove the pan from the heat, drain into a bowl, and let cool.

5. To serve, arrange a whole poached pear on a serving plate and drizzle it with the reduced poaching syrup. Garnish with mint leaves and raspberries, if desired. Serve any remaining syrup separately.

Fancy Poached Pears with Fillings

➤ *Makes 6 servings* ◄

*I*f my version of Poached Pears (page 184) is simple, just look at what you can do when you want to fancy them up!

You can roll the pears in delicious toasted hazelnuts and serve them whole. Or you can drizzle the pears with a fabulously rich double chocolate sauce. Or you can let out all the stops and halve them, then fill the centers with contrasting layers of pastry cream and chocolate sauce.

To save time, the pastry cream can be made in advance and stored in the refrigerator, as can the chocolate sauce. (You will need to rewarm the sauce before you use it, of course.) In fact, the pears can be prepared in advance as well. Store them in the refrigerator in the poaching liquid that you haven't yet reduced. When you're getting ready to serve the pears, simmer the liquid as directed on page 184.

6 slightly underripe Bartlett pears

♥ Hazelnut coating:

2 cups skinned, toasted hazelnuts, chopped
　(see Tip: To Skin Hazelnuts, page 172)

♥ Double chocolate sauce:

3 ounces high-quality semisweet chocolate,
　chopped

3 ounces high-quality milk chocolate, chopped

3 tablespoons heavy cream

½ recipe Pastry Cream (page 55), cooled, as
　accompaniment

1. Poach the pears according to the directions on page 184. Drain and cool them, and reduce
　and reserve the poaching liquid.

Make the hazelnut-coated poached pears:

2. Brush the whole poached pears with the reserved poaching syrup, then roll the pears, 1 at a time, in the chopped hazelnuts to cover all the surfaces.

Make the double chocolate sauce:

3. In a ceramic or glass bowl covered with plastic wrap, heat the chocolates with the cream in a microwave oven on High for 30-second intervals, stirring after each interval, until smooth.
4. To serve, put a whole poached pear on each dessert plate and ladle the hot chocolate sauce over the top. Serve the remaining chocolate sauce separately.

Make the pastry cream— and chocolate sauce—filled pears:

5. Have the pastry cream and the double chocolate sauce ready. If desired, brush each pear with the reduced syrup, then roll in toasted chopped hazelnuts. Slice each poached pear in half. Place level tablespoons of the pastry cream and then the chocolate sauce over the middle of each pear half. Transfer carefully to a dessert plate.

Baked Apple in Butter Crust

Makes 4 servings

The baked apple is simple and comforting and as easy to do as almost any dessert I know. This apple is a special-occasion treat of pudding-filled poached apples, baked to a golden turn in a sweet, buttery crust. All the components of the recipe can be done in stages ahead of time. You can decorate the apples as fancifully or simply as you like with dough cut-outs.

Be sure to reserve the poaching liquid. It's wonderful when reduced and served over cut-up fresh fruit or as a sauce over ice cream.

Equipment Needed: ★ BAKING PARCHMENT ★ FLUTED PASTRY CUTTER ★ MELON BALLER

❦ Sweet pastry:

2 cups all-purpose flour

1½ tablespoons sugar

½ teaspoon salt

8 tablespoons (1 stick) cold unsalted butter, cut
    into chunks

1 large egg yolk, well chilled

½ teaspoon pure vanilla extract

1 to 2 tablespoons ice water

❦ Apples:

2 cups apricot nectar

½ cup firmly packed light brown sugar

1 teaspoon ground cinnamon

¼ teaspoon ground cloves

4 medium-size tart apples, such as Gala,
    Fuji, or Granny Smith

❦ Filling:

1 small package vanilla pudding (not the
    instant variety), cooked according to
    package directions

1½ cups firmly packed dark brown sugar

❦ Eggwash:

1 large egg, lightly beaten

Make the sweet pastry:

1. In a large bowl, whisk together the flour, sugar, and salt. With a pastry cutter, cut in the butter until the mixture is coarsely textured with small, irregular flakes and bits the size of small peas.

2. In a cup, stir together the egg yolk, vanilla, and ice water. Sprinkle the yolk mixture over the flour mixture, a little at a time, stirring with a fork, until the dough just holds together. Gather the dough and divide it into 4 equal balls. Flatten each ball into a disk, wrap it in plastic wrap, and refrigerate for 1 hour.

Prepare the apples:

3. In a medium-size saucepan over medium-low heat, combine the apricot nectar, brown sugar, cinnamon, and cloves, stirring until the sugar is dissolved.

4. Meanwhile, peel the apples, halve them crosswise. With a melon baller or a small, sharp knife, core the insides, leaving a ½-inch shell. Add the apples to the poaching liquid and poach them at a bare simmer for 10 to 12 minutes, or until they can be pierced with a knife. Do not overcook them; the apples should still be rather firm at the end of the cooking time. Remove the apples from the poaching liquid and let cool, rounded sides up, on a wire rack. (If desired, reserve the poaching liquid for another use.)

Assemble the apples:

5. On a well-floured surface, roll out each disk of dough into a circle about 10 inches in diameter. Using a fluted pastry cutter, cut a triangle shape out of each circular dough piece, reserving the scraps for later.

6. Blot the apples with paper towels to remove any remaining moisture and pair up matching halves. Line a baking sheet with baking parchment.

7. Fill the cavity of each of the apples with 1 heaping teaspoon each of pudding and brown sugar. Cover each apple with its matching filled half. Center each apple on a triangle of dough.

8. Press 2 tablespoons of brown sugar onto each apple, letting any excess fall onto the dough. Enclose the apple in the dough, sealing the dough at the bottom by wetting your fingertips with cold water and pressing the edges together.

9. Reflour the work surface, roll out the reserved dough scraps, and with the pastry cutter or a small, sharp knife, cut out leaf shapes and stems and attach them decoratively to the dough, brushing the dough first with water to make the pieces adhere. Brush the dough all over with eggwash.

10. Transfer the apples to the prepared baking sheet and place in the freezer for at least 30 minutes.

11. Preheat the oven to 400 degrees F.

12. Bake the apples for 25 to 30 minutes, then tent the tops of the apples with aluminum foil and bake 10 minutes more. Remove the apples to a wire rack and let cool for 30 minutes before serving.

Baked Pear in Butter Crust

> ⇒ *Makes 4 servings* ⇐

*T*his is a variation of my very special baked apples, except that this time nuts and chocolate cream are the surprise when you cut into these almost-too-beautiful-to-eat pears! I love the way they look, and you'll love the gasps of delight from your dinner guests when you present these at the end of a gala meal.

The fruit you use should be firm but not rock solid. That can be difficult because pears are often unready for use when you buy them at the market. You can ripen them in either a plastic or a brown paper bag with other ethylene-producing fruit such as apples or bananas.

⇒ *Equipment Needed:*
- ★ BAKING SHEET
- ★ BAKING PARCHMENT
- ★ MELON BALLER
- ★ FLUTED PASTRY CUTTER

1 recipe Sweet Pastry dough, page 188

❦ Pears:

2 cups apricot nectar

1 cup firmly packed dark brown sugar

1 teaspoon ground cinnamon

¼ teaspoon ground cloves

¼ teaspoon ground nutmeg

4 ripe but firm pears

❦ Nut filling:

½ cup coarsely chopped pecans, toasted

3 tablespoons honey

1 tablespoon fresh lemon juice

2 teaspoons pure vanilla extract

❦ Dark chocolate cream

8 ounces semisweet chocolate, coarsely chopped

¼ cup heavy cream

❧ White chocolate cream:

8 ounces white chocolate, coarsely chopped
¼ cup heavy cream

½ cup dark brown sugar

❧ Eggwash:

1 large egg, lightly beaten

1. Prepare the Sweet Pastry dough and chill according to the directions on page 188.

Prepare the pears:

2. In a medium-size saucepan over medium-low heat, combine the apricot nectar, brown sugar, cinnamon, cloves, and nutmeg, stirring until the sugar is dissolved.

3. Peel the pears, halve them lengthwise, and with a melon baller or a small, sharp knife, core the insides, leaving a ½-inch shell. Carefully carve out the core ends. Add the pear halves to the poaching liquid and poach them at a simmer for 10 to 12 minutes. Take care not to overcook them; the pears should still be firm at the end of the cooking time. Remove the pears from the poaching liquid and let cool, rounded side up, on a wire rack.

Make the nut filling:

4. In a small bowl, combine the pecans, honey, lemon juice, and vanilla.

Make the dark chocolate cream and white chocolate cream:

5. In a ceramic or glass bowl covered with plastic wrap, melt the semisweet chocolate with the cream on High in a microwave oven for 30-second intervals, stirring after each interval, until smooth. Set aside to cool. In a separate ceramic or glass bowl, melt the white chocolate with the cream in the same manner.

Assemble the pears:

6. On a well-floured surface, roll out each ball of pastry into a circle about 10 inches in diameter. Using a flute pastry cutter, cut a triangle shape out of each circular dough piece, reserving the scraps for later.

7. Blot the pears dry with paper towels to remove any remaining moisture and pair up the matching halves. Line a baking sheet with baking parchment.

8. Fill the cavity of each pear half with 1 heaping teaspoon each of nut filling, dark chocolate cream, and white chocolate cream. Cover each pear with its matching filled half. Center each pear on a piece of dough.

9. Press 2 tablespoons of brown sugar onto each pear, letting any excess fall onto the dough. Enclose the pears in the dough, decorate them with pastry cutouts of leaf shapes, and brush the dough all over with the eggwash. Put the pears on the prepared baking sheet and place them in freezer for at least 30 minutes.

10. Preheat the oven to 400 degrees F.

11. Bake the pears, standing upright, for 25 to 30 minutes, then tent the tops of the pears with aluminum foil and bake 10 minutes more. Remove the pears to a wire rack and let cool for 30 minutes before serving.

12. If desired, serve the pears with any remaining chocolate cream, or ladle chocolate cream onto each serving plate, and then set a pear on top of it.

Debbi's Truffle Cake

➤ *Makes 6 to 8 servings* ◄

*W*hen you want a cake that's truly special, that celebrates the significance of an occasion like a birthday or anniversary in an unforgettable way, look no further. Here's the cake that says it all.

This cake bakes in a loaf pan and looks quite innocent when sliced and ready for serving on a plate. But don't be fooled. One taste tells you there's nothing innocent about this cake at all. With lots of chocolate, butter, and eggs, only a trace of flour, and a touch of cinnamon, this cake is dense and glorious to eat. It's not by accident that this is called truffle— as in the chocolate confection—cake! I serve it drizzled with chocolate glaze, although if you feel that's too intense, you can serve a little unsweetened whipped cream on the side.

➤ *Equipment Needed:* ★ 9 BY 5 BY 3-INCH LOAF PAN ★ ELECTRIC MIXER

♥ Cake:

8 tablespoons (1 stick) unsalted butter, cut into pieces

6 ounces semisweet chocolate, chopped

3 large eggs, separated, the whites at room temperature

²/₃ cup sugar

¹/₃ cup all-purpose flour

2 teaspoons ground cinnamon

♥ Glaze:

¹/₃ cup heavy cream

8 ounces semisweet chocolate, chopped

1. Preheat the oven to 325 degrees F. Butter and lightly flour the loaf pan.

Make the cake:

2. In a heavy saucepan over low heat, melt the butter with the chocolate, stirring until smooth. Remove the pan from the heat.
3. Put the egg yolks in a bowl and beat until combined using the electric mixer on medium speed. Gradually add the sugar and beat for 4 to 5 minutes, until thick and pale. Whisk together the flour and cinnamon, and beat in until combined. Slowly beat in the melted chocolate mixture until combined.
4. In another bowl, beat the egg whites until stiff using the electric mixer on medium speed with clean beaters. Gently fold half of the beaten whites into the chocolate mixture until combined, then fold in the remaining whites. Spoon the batter into the prepared pan.
5. Fill a 2-quart baking pan halfway with hot water and place on the bottom rack of the oven. Bake the cake on the middle rack for 50 to 55 minutes, until a toothpick inserted in the center comes out clean. Remove the cake to a wire rack and cool for 10 minutes. Run a thin knife blade around the edge of the pan to loosen the sides of the cake and remove the cake. Let the cake cool to room temperature, then wrap it in plastic wrap and refrigerate for at least 2 hours.

Make the glaze:

6. In a ceramic or glass bowl covered with plastic wrap, heat the cream with the chocolate on High in a microwave oven for 30-second intervals, stirring after each interval, until smooth.
7. To serve, cut the cake into slices and serve drizzled with the chocolate glaze. Serve any remaining glaze separately.

Triple Truffle Cake

⋗ *Makes one 10 by 5-inch triple-layer cake* ⋘

*T*his three-layer truffle cake is enriched with ground almonds, soaked with coffee syrup, and gilded with a dense frosting. It's a symphony of taste and texture.

If you don't have a pastry bag, you can still prepare this special occasion cake by spreading the frosting over the sides and top.

⋗ *Equipment Needed:* ★ 10 BY 15-INCH JELLY-ROLL PAN ★ BAKING PARCHMENT ★ ELECTRIC MIXER ★ PASTRY BAG (OPTIONAL)

❦ Chocolate frosting:

1 cup heavy cream

2 tablespoons (½ stick) unsalted butter

1½ tablespoons light corn syrup

12 ounces semisweet chocolate, chopped

❦ Cake:

4 ounces semisweet chocolate, chopped

6 tablespoons (¾ stick) unsalted butter, softened

½ cup sugar, divided

4 large eggs, at room temperature, separated

4 ounces toasted blanched almonds, finely ground

⅓ cup plain bread crumbs

½ teaspoon cream of tartar

❦ Coffee syrup:

¼ cup strong coffee

¼ cup sugar

1 tablespoon coffee liqueur

❦ Garnish:

Chocolate leaves (optional)

Make the chocolate frosting:

1. In a medium-size saucepan over medium heat, bring the cream, butter, and corn syrup to a boil. Remove the pan from the heat and pour the hot cream mixture over the chocolate in a bowl. Let stand for 5 minutes, then whisk until smooth. Cover loosely and refrigerate, stirring occasionally, until thick enough to spread.

Make the cake:

2. Preheat the oven to 325 degrees F. Line the jelly-roll pan with baking parchment and butter the paper.

3. In a ceramic or glass bowl covered with plastic wrap, melt the chocolate on High in a microwave oven for 30-second intervals, stirring after each interval, until smooth. Set aside to cool.

4. Put the butter and half of the sugar in a bowl and cream together using the electric mixer on medium speed. Add the cooled chocolate and beat until combined. Add the eggs, 1 at a time, beating for 20 seconds after each addition. Scrape down the bowl. Add the almonds and crumbs and beat on low speed until combined.

5. In another bowl, beat the egg whites until frothy using the mixer and clean beaters. Add the cream of tartar and the remaining sugar, a little at a time, and beat until stiff peaks form. Fold one-third of the beaten whites into the batter to lighten it. Fold the remaining whites in until no streaks of white remain.

6. Place the batter in the prepared pan and bake for 20 to 25 minutes, or until a toothpick inserted in the center comes out clean. Remove the pan to a wire rack and let cool for 10 minutes. Invert the pan onto a large wire rack and remove the paper. Turn the cake right side up and cool to room temperature.

Make the coffee syrup:

7. In a small saucepan, combine the coffee, sugar, and liqueur over medium heat, stirring until the sugar is dissolved. Set aside to cool.

Assemble the cake:

8. Brush the cake with the coffee syrup. Slice the cake into thirds crosswise, making three 5 by 10-inch layers. Set one of the layers on a serving plate and spread a thin film of frosting over the top. Set another cake layer on top and spread it with a thin film of frosting. Top with the remaining cake. Spread or pipe the remaining frosting with a pastry bag fitted with a ribbon tip in a decorative design over the sides and top of the cake. Garnish as desired.

Truffle Pie

⇒ *Makes 12 servings* ⇐

*M*ention the word "truffle," and you could be referring to one of nature's most expensive ingredients or to a luxurious chocolate confection. Like a good truffle, this pie is rich and silky and intense with the flavor of good chocolate. Just a thin slice makes the most wonderful ending to an elegant meal.

As extravagant as this pie looks and tastes, it may be one of the simplest and quickest recipes to prepare in this book. The crust comes together in a food processor, and the pie, once filled, requires no baking at all.

⇒ *Equipment Needed:*
  ★ FOOD PROCESSOR FITTED WITH METAL BLADE
  ★ 8- OR 9-INCH TART PAN WITH REMOVABLE BOTTOM
  ★ ELECTRIC MIXER ★ PASTRY BAG (OPTIONAL)

❦ Crust:

1½ cups pecans, toasted
6 tablespoons all-purpose flour
⅓ cup firmly packed dark brown sugar

½ teaspoon ground nutmeg
2 tablespoons cold unsalted butter, cut into pieces

♥ Filling:

1¾ cups heavy cream
1 pound semisweet chocolate, chopped

2 large egg yolks, at room temperature
1 tablespoon pure vanilla extract

♥ Whipped cream:

1 cup heavy cream, chilled

3 tablespoons powdered sugar

♥ Garnish:

Grated semisweet chocolate

1. Preheat the oven to 350 degrees F.

Make the crust:

2. Combine the pecans, flour, brown sugar, nutmeg, and butter, in a food processor and pulse until the nuts are crushed and the butter is incorporated. Remove from processor and press the crust over the bottom and up the sides of the pan. Bake for 15 minutes; then set aside on a rack to cool.

Make the filling:

3. In a heavy saucepan, heat the cream until it just begins to bubble around the edges; be careful not to let it scorch.
4. In a double boiler set over barely simmering water, melt the chocolate, stirring until smooth. Gradually add the hot cream to the melted chocolate, stirring constantly to combine. Stir in the egg yolks and vanilla until fully blended. Cook over low heat until thickened and hot, 8 to 10 minutes. Pour the filling into the prebaked crust and chill for at least 4 hours.

Make the whipped cream:

5. Put the cream and powdered sugar in a chilled bowl and beat with the electric mixer on medium speed until stiff peaks form.
6. Before serving, pipe the whipped cream with a pastry bag over the filling in a crosshatch pattern or spoon it on decoratively. Sprinkle the grated chocolate over all.
7. Remove the sides of the pan and transfer the pie to a plate for serving.

Cappuccino Truffle Mousse Pie

≽ *Makes 12 servings* ≼

*T*he drama of Truffle Pie (page 196) lies in its intensely flavored chocolate filling. One day I was wondering how to lighten the filling but still keep the exquisite richness of that wonderful pie. I added whipped cream to the cappuccino-flavored top layer. Then I added a nutty crust and a white chocolate drizzle over all.

This dessert is a showstopper, but it's easy to make. In fact, it has to be made in advance to allow the filling, a basic mousse preparation, to chill.

≽ *Equipment Needed:*
★ 9-INCH TART PAN WITH REMOVABLE BOTTOM
★ ELECTRIC MIXER

❖ Crust:

2 cups skinned hazelnuts, toasted (See Tip: To Skin Hazelnuts, page 172)

4 tablespoons all-purpose flour

⅓ cup firmly packed light brown sugar

½ teaspoon ground nutmeg

2 tablespoons cold unsalted butter, cut into pieces

❖ Mousse filling:

2 large egg yolks, at room temperature

1⅓ cups heavy cream

12 ounces semisweet chocolate, chopped

1 tablespoon pure vanilla extract

2 tablespoons instant coffee crystals dissolved in 1 tablespoon hot water

⅔ cup chilled heavy cream, beaten until stiff

❖ Garnish:

1 cup heavy cream, divided

8 ounces white chocolate, chopped

3 tablespoons powdered sugar

1. Preheat the oven to 350 degrees F. Butter the tart pan and set aside.

Make the crust:

2. Combine the nuts, flour, brown sugar, nutmeg, and butter in a food processor and pulse until the nuts are finely ground and the butter is incorporated. Press the crust over the bottom and up the sides of the tart pan. Bake for 15 minutes, then set aside on a rack to cool.

Make the filling:

3. In the top of a double boiler set over barely simmering water, whisk together the egg yolks. Whisk in the cream and cook, stirring, until thickened, 8 to 10 minutes. Stir in the chopped chocolate and vanilla, and whisk until the chocolate is melted and the mixture is smooth.

4. Pour ⅔ of the warm chocolate filling into the prebaked crust, then refrigerate the pie for 1 hour.

5. While the remaining chocolate filling is still warm, add the dissolved coffee mixture and whisk until smooth. Cover with plastic wrap and let cool on a wire rack for 30 minutes.

6. Fold the whipped cream into the cooled cappuccino mixture until no white streaks remain. Spoon the filling over the chilled chocolate filling in the pie shell, spreading it evenly, and refrigerate the pie again for 4 hours.

Make the garnish:

7. In a ceramic or glass bowl covered with plastic wrap, heat ⅓ cup of the heavy cream with the white chocolate on High in a microwave oven for 30-second intervals, stirring after each interval, until smooth.

8. Put the remaining ⅔ cup of cream and the powdered sugar in a chilled bowl and beat using the electric mixer until stiff peaks form.

Assemble the pie:

9. Garnish the top of the pie with dollops of the whipped cream, then drizzle the white chocolate cream decoratively over the cream and pie.

> *Tip:* USING A SQUEEZE BOTTLE WITH CHOCOLATE CREAM TO GARNISH

Using a squeeze bottle is the easiest way to create a design with a melted chocolate garnish. Simply put warm chocolate cream in the bottle and squeeze gently over the surface of the dessert. If you have any leftover cream, store the bottle in the refrigerator. To reuse, simply heat the bottle in hot water until the cream pours again. Make everyday desserts special by drizzling chocolate cream prettily over a piece of bundt or pound cake or, easier still, a scoop or two of frozen yogurt.

Pecan Lily Pads

> *Makes 18* <

The term "lily pad" has always summoned up an image so beautiful to me that I felt destined to use it as the title of one of my special-occasion desserts. I call these a dessert, but they're really confections—nuts, caramel, and chocolate. I absolutely adore these nuggets of delight (and the macadamia nut variation that follows).

Pay attention when cooling the caramel. You want to be able to shape it with your hands, which means it must be cool, but it must not be so cold that it hardens and sets. Here, practice will make perfect.

> *Equipment Needed:* ★ BAKING SHEET ★ PASTRY BRUSH

2 tablespoons butter
¼ cup heavy cream
¾ cup sugar
¼ cup water
½ teaspoon fresh lemon juice
1 recipe Double Chocolate Sauce
    (page 186)

❦ Garnish:

72 toasted pecan halves, plus additional chopped pecans, toasted

1. Line a baking sheet with aluminum foil
   and spray with nonstick cooking spray.
   Set aside.

Make the caramel:

2. Follow the directions on page 176, Steps 4 and 5. Transfer the caramel to a bowl, cover,
   and cool on a rack for 15 to 20 minutes, or until firm enough to form into a ball with your
   fingertips.
3. Prepare the Double Chocolate Sauce according to the directions on page 187.

Make the candies:

4. On the prepared baking sheet, arrange a cross-shaped cluster of 4 pecan halves. Scoop 1
   heaping teaspoon of the caramel and press it over the center of the nut cluster, letting the
   ends of some of the nuts remain exposed. Spoon a level teaspoon of the warm chocolate
   sauce over the caramel, spreading it smooth and letting it drip over the candy. Sprinkle
   chopped nuts over the warm chocolate.
5. Continue to make candies with the remaining ingredients in the same way. When done,
   refrigerate the candies, covered, on the baking sheet for 30 minutes. Store any remaining
   candies in layers separated by sheets of wax paper in an airtight container.

Macadamia Lily Pads

*L*ily pads made with macadamia nuts are special enough, but I've added a little something extra: Instead of topping the nut clusters with caramel and double chocolate sauce, I've used caramel and peanut butter fudge sauce. The combination is fantastic! In fact, when the girls and I make lily pads, we make a batch of each and serve them together. You guessed it—there are never any left!

➤ *Equipment Needed:* ★ PASTRY BRUSH (FOR CARAMEL) ★ BAKING SHEET

1 recipe Caramel (page 202)

❦ Peanut butter fudge sauce:

6 ounces high-quality semisweet chocolate, chopped

3 tablespoons heavy cream

2 tablespoons creamy peanut butter

About 100 whole macadamia nuts, plus additional, chopped for garnish

1. Spray a foil-lined baking sheet with nonstick cooking spray and set aside.
2. Make caramel as directed on page 176 and cool it as instructed in Step 2 on page 202.

Make peanut butter fudge sauce:

3. In a ceramic or glass bowl covered with plastic wrap, heat the chocolate with the cream and peanut butter on High in a microwave oven for 30-second intervals, stirring after each interval, until smooth.
4. Make lily pads, using 5 or 6 nuts, depending upon the size, for each cluster, arranging in a circular pattern on the baking sheet. Spoon the caramel and the peanut butter fudge sauce over tops. Garnish with chopped macadamia nuts, cool, and store as directed on page 202.

Chapter 9

Icebox Desserts

AN ICEBOX DESSERT WASN'T even a possibility in the United States until the turn of the twentieth century when mechanical refrigeration entered the American home. Enter icebox desserts, and aren't we all better off for them?

There are icebox pies and icebox cookies (also called refrigerator cookies), but my all-time favorite, hands down, is Baked Alaska—layers of cake and ice cream covered with meringue and then baked. It may not seem like much of a feat to bake ice cream, but when it was accomplished by the scientist Benjamin Thompson (1753–1814), it created an incredible stir. And the dessert still impresses. My version of it pairs chocolate and vanilla for a very dramatic presentation, and I've created adorable individualized Baked Alaskas as well.

Whether you're serving a kid-friendly dessert, such as Peanut Butter Chocolate Mud Pie (page 214), which needs no baking at all, or Fudge Mousse (page 218), or any of the others in this group of seven icebox desserts, you can feel very secure about one thing: the timing. With icebox desserts there's no last-minute fussing: These treats *must* be prepared in advance!

Debbi's Layered Ice-Cream Cake

⇒ *Makes 16 servings* ⇐

I've loved ice-cream cake since I first tasted it as a little girl. The sponge cake I've included here is very light and scented with almonds. Be careful not to overbeat the batter; you want the cake to be as light and airy as possible.

I like vanilla ice cream with this, but coffee or cappuccino ice cream is good, too, especially for mocha lovers.

Like the Baked Alaskas (pages 208 and 211), this is a wonderful dessert for entertaining. There's no last-minute fussing because it *has* to be made in advance!

⇒ *Equipment Needed:* ★ 9-INCH SPRINGFORM PAN ★ ELECTRIC MIXER

❦ Sponge cake:

6 large eggs

¾ cup sifted cake flour (not self-rising, see
   Tip: Self-rising Flour, page 35)

½ cup cornstarch

8 tablespoons (1 stick) unsalted butter, melted

1½ teaspoons pure vanilla extract

¾ teaspoon pure almond extract

¾ cup sugar

¼ cup blanched almonds, toasted and finely
   ground

❦ Chocolate fudge:

1 cup heavy cream

2 tablespoons sugar

12 ounces semisweet chocolate, chopped into
   small pieces

1 pint vanilla ice cream, softened in the refrigerator 30 to 45 minutes before use

❦ Garnish:

Whipped cream

1. Preheat the oven to 350 degrees F. Butter and flour the springform pan. Place the eggs in a bowl, run hot tap water over them to cover. Let stand 15 minutes.

Make the spongecake:

2. In a bowl, whisk together the flour and cornstarch. In another bowl, stir together the melted butter and vanilla and almond extracts.
3. Put the warm eggs and sugar in a large bowl and beat using the electric mixer on high speed until triple in volume, about 5 minutes. Sift the flour mixture in thirds over the beaten eggs and fold in gently. Fold in the ground almonds gently, then the butter mixture until thoroughly combined. Be careful not to overmix or the egg whites will deflate.
4. Pour the batter immediately into the prepared pan and bake on the middle rack of the oven for 30 to 35 minutes, until the top is golden brown and the center springs back slightly when pressed. Do not open the oven door before the cake looks done or it may fall.
5. Remove the cake from the oven to a wire rack and cool for 10 minutes. Run a thin knife around the inside edge of the pan and remove the sides. Invert the cake and remove the bottom of the pan. Turn the cake right side up on wire rack and finish cooling it.
6. Wash and dry the springform pan for later use.

Make the chocolate fudge:

7. In a ceramic or glass bowl covered with plastic wrap, heat the cream, sugar, and chocolate on High in a microwave oven for 30-second intervals, stirring after each interval, until smooth. Set aside.

Assemble the cake:

8. With a serrated knife, cut the cake horizontally into 2 layers. Place the bottom layer back into the clean springform pan, pour half the fudge over it, and smooth the surface. Place the pan in the freezer for 30 minutes.
9. Spread all the vanilla ice cream over the chocolate fudge in the chilled pan. Top with the remaining cake layer and spread it with the remaining chocolate fudge. (If the fudge has become too thick to spread, warm it slightly and whisk until smooth.) Cover the pan with aluminum foil and freeze the cake for at least 2 hours.
10. To serve, remove the sides of the springform pan and place the cake on a serving plate. Pipe whipped cream decoratively on the cake and serve immediately.

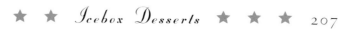

Baked Alaska

*H*ow Baked Alaska—just its name alone is terrific—came to be a classic dessert is very easy to understand, with its cold, firm ice cream on a base of tender cake, encased in a meringue shell that is golden on the outside and creamy within. The hot-cold, crisp-soft textures are a magic combination.

I've tasted Baked Alaskas with several layers of different ice creams, but this version is a vision in black and white: yellow cake topped with chocolate cream topped with chocolate-chunk vanilla ice cream topped with chocolate ice cream topped with meringue.

Though it may look intimidating, this is actually a fun, very easy dessert to make. I love to serve it when I'm entertaining because it looks so elegant and it's the perfect make-ahead dessert. In fact, it *has* to be prepared in advance in order to set. I start two days in advance, then all I have to do before serving is prepare the meringue, spread it over the ice cream, and bake. Then it can't wait, and neither should you—to taste it.

Baked Alaska Countdown

2 days before:
★ Layer the chocolate and vanilla ice creams in the bowl, cover, and freeze.
★ Bake the cake and let it cool. Store wrapped in plastic wrap and foil.
★ Make the coffee syrup.

The day before:
★ Make the chocolate cream and add to the ice cream layers.
★ Add cake layer, wrap well, and refreeze.

Just before serving:
★ Preheat the oven.
★ Make the meringue.
★ Complete the Baked Alaska.

❦ Ice-Cream Layers:

1 pint premium chocolate ice cream, softened in the refrigerator for 30 minutes before using

2 pints premium vanilla ice cream, softened in the refrigerator for 30 minutes before using

4 ounces semisweet chocolate, chopped into small pieces

❦ Cake:

4 large eggs, at room temperature, separated

³/₄ cup plus 2 tablespoons sugar

2 teaspoons pure vanilla extract

¹/₄ teaspoon cream of tartar

³/₄ cup cake flour (not *self-rising*, see *Tip: Self-rising Flour, page 35*)

¹/₄ teaspoon salt

4 tablespoons (¹/₂ stick) unsalted butter, melted and cooled slightly

❦ Coffee syrup:

¹/₄ cup strong brewed coffee

¹/₄ cup sugar

1 tablespoon coffee liqueur

❦ Chocolate cream:

¹/₂ cup heavy cream

8 ounces semisweet chocolate, chopped into small pieces

❦ Meringue:

6 large egg whites, at room temperature

¹/₂ teaspoon cream of tartar

³/₄ cup sugar

1. Line the bowl with aluminum foil, extending it 2 inches all the way around the rim.
2. Spread a 1-inch-thick layer of chocolate ice cream over the bottom of the foil-lined bowl. Place the bowl in the freezer while you prepare the vanilla ice cream.
3. Stir the chocolate pieces into the softened vanilla ice cream, then spread all of it over the chocolate layer in the bowl and smooth the top. Cover the bowl and return it to the freezer for about 2 hours, until the vanilla ice cream is firm.

Make the cake:

4. Preheat the oven to 350 degrees F. Butter and flour the cake pan.
5. Put the egg yolks and ¾ cup sugar in a bowl and beat on high speed using the electric mixer for about 5 minutes, or until light. Turn the speed to low and beat in the vanilla.
6. In another bowl, beat the egg whites until frothy using the electric mixer and clean beaters. Add the cream of tartar and beat until soft peaks form. Gradually add the remaining 2 tablespoons sugar, beating until stiff peaks form. Fold this mixture into the yolk mixture.
7. Sift the cake flour and salt over the batter and gently fold them in. Drizzle in the melted butter and fold it in until it is fully incorporated.
8. Pour the batter into the prepared cake pan and bake on the middle rack of the oven for 25 to 28 minutes, until a cake tester inserted in the center comes out clean. Remove the pan to a wire rack to cool for 10 minutes, then turn the cake out onto the rack to cool to lukewarm.

While the cake is baking, make the coffee syrup:

9. In a small, heavy saucepan on medium heat, stir the coffee with the sugar to dissolve it, remove the pan from the heat, and stir in the coffee liqueur. Brush the syrup over the warm cake.

Make the chocolate cream:

10. In a ceramic or glass bowl covered with plastic wrap, heat the cream with the chocolate on High in a microwave oven for 30-second intervals, stirring after each interval, until smooth. Let cool to room temperature.
11. Remove the bowl of ice cream from the freezer. Spread the chocolate cream evenly over the ice cream, then top the chocolate cream with the cake layer. Cover the bowl and return it to the freezer for about 1 hour, or until the chocolate is firm.
12. Preheat the oven to 475 degrees F.

13. Put the egg whites in a bowl and beat them until frothy using the electric mixer on high speed. Add the cream of tartar and beat in the sugar, a little at a time, until glossy, stiff peaks form.

Assemble and bake:

14. Remove the bowl from the freezer and turn the ice-cream-and-cake mold out of the bowl by inverting it onto a heatproof serving plate. Remove and discard the foil. With a metal spatula, spread the meringue decoratively over the dessert, being careful to cover the ice cream completely.

15. Bake the dessert for 5 to 7 minutes, or until the meringue browns lightly. Serve immediately.

Baby Baked Alaskas

Makes 6 servings

*I*f Baked Alaska is special, just imagine your own individual one. These babies, as I call them, are charming, true special-occasion desserts, and as much fun to make as they are to eat. I've used chocolate cake, chocolate cream, and chocolate ice cream, and I also like to serve them with the remaining chocolate cream on the side. Like my more classic chocolate-and-vanilla version on page 208, these are a perfect make-ahead desserts. If you're serving these to children, it's a good idea to divide each Baby Baked Alaska in half.

Equipment Needed: ★ SIX 4- TO 5-INCH ROUND BOWLS (12-OUNCE CAPACITY EACH) ★ 10 BY 15-INCH JELLY-ROLL PAN ★ ELECTRIC MIXER

♥ Cake:

½ cup unsweetened cocoa powder

½ cup boiling water

1½ cup sifted cake flour (not self-rising, see
    Tip: Self-rising Flour, page 35)

1½ teaspoons baking powder

½ teaspoon baking soda

½ teaspoon salt

1½ cups firmly packed light brown sugar

⅓ cup vegetable oil

2 large eggs

1½ teaspoons pure vanilla extract

½ cup milk

3 pints premium chocolate ice cream, softened
    in the refrigerator for 30 minutes before
    using

♥ Chocolate cream:

1 cup heavy cream

8 ounces semisweet chocolate, cut into medium
    chunks

♥ Meringue:

9 large egg whites, at room temperature

¾ teaspoon cream of tartar

1¼ cups sugar

1. Preheat the oven to 350 degrees F. Line each bowl with aluminum foil, extending it 2 inches all the way around the rim. Butter and flour the jelly-roll pan.

Make the cake:

2. In a small bowl, whisk together the cocoa and boiling water until smooth. Set aside to cool.

3. Put the cake flour, baking powder, baking soda, and salt in a medium bowl and whisk together.

4. Put the brown sugar and vegetable oil in a bowl and beat using the electric mixer on medium speed until smooth. Add the eggs, 1 at a time, beating for 20 seconds after each addition. Add the vanilla and cooled cocoa mixture and beat until smooth.

5. Scrape down the bowl with a rubber spatula. Add the flour mixture in thirds, alternating with the milk, and beat for 45 seconds after each addition.

6. Scrape the batter into the prepared pan and smooth the top. Bake on the middle rack of the oven for 20 to 25 minutes, until a cake tester inserted in the center comes out clean. Remove the pan to a wire rack to cool for 10 minutes. Turn the cake out of the pan onto the rack and let it cool completely.

7. Invert a lined serving bowl onto the cake and, using it as your guide, cut around the rim with a sharp knife to make a round to fit inside the bottom of a serving bowl. Cut out 5 more rounds in the same manner and set aside.

8. Spoon 1 cup of softened ice cream into the bottom of each serving bowl and smooth the surface. Cover tightly and return to the freezer.

Make the chocolate cream:

9. In a ceramic or glass bowl covered with plastic wrap, heat the cream with the chocolate on High in a microwave oven for 30-second intervals, stirring after each interval, until smooth. Let cool slightly.

10. Remove 1 bowl at a time from the freezer and spread the surface of the ice cream with about 2 tablespoons of the chocolate cream. Top with 1 of the reserved cake rounds. Cover with foil, return the bowl to the freezer, and repeat with the 5 remaining bowls. Freeze for at least 2 hours, or until firm. Transfer the remaining chocolate cream to a serving bowl.

Make the meringue:

11. Put the egg whites in a large bowl and beat until frothy using the electric mixer on high speed. Add the cream of tartar and the sugar, a little at a time, and beat until glossy, stiff peaks form.

12. Preheat the oven to 475 degrees F.

13. Remove the bowls from the freezer and, using the foil overhangs, remove each dessert from its bowl. Remove and discard the foil. Set the molds on a baking sheet, ice cream side up, and spread meringue over the top and sides, swirling it decoratively with a rubber spatula or pastry bag fitted with a decorative tip.

14. Bake the desserts for 4 to 6 minutes, or until the meringue browns lightly. Transfer the desserts immediately with a spatula to individual dessert plates and serve with the remaining chocolate cream as an accompaniment.

Peanut Butter Chocolate Mud Pie

⮞ *Makes 12 servings* ⮜

*T*his is a no-bake pie with an intense, luscious peanut flavor. I've called for a peanut butter cookie crumb crust, but if a chocolate and peanut butter combination is more to your liking, go right ahead and substitute an equal amount of chocolate wafer crumbs. A chocolate crust would also very nicely echo the rich chocolate garnish.

By the way, freezing the crust after you've pressed it into the pie plate is a little trick I discovered one day that actually helps prevent the crust from becoming soggy. I do it with all my unbaked crumb crusts.

⮞ *Equipment Needed:* ★ 9-INCH DEEP-DISH PIE PAN   ★ ELECTRIC MIXER

❦ Crust:

2 cups peanut butter cookie crumbs (eighteen 2-inch cookies)

½ cup finely chopped pecans, toasted

2 tablespoons sugar

4 tablespoons unsalted butter, melted

❦ Filling:

1½ cups heavy cream, chilled

12 ounces cream cheese, softened

¾ cup superfine sugar

1 cup smooth peanut butter

1 tablespoon pure vanilla extract

❦ Chocolate cream:

¾ cup semisweet chocolate chips

2 tablespoons heavy cream

½ cup coarsely chopped roasted unsalted peanuts, for sprinkling

Make the crust:

1. In a large bowl, combine the cookie crumbs, pecans, and sugar. Stir in the melted butter until combined. Press the crust over the bottom and up the sides of the pie pan. Put the pan in the freezer for 1 hour.

Make the filling:

2. Put the heavy cream in a chilled bowl and beat using an electric mixer on medium speed until stiff peaks form.
3. Put the cream cheese and sugar in a bowl and beat until smooth using the mixer on medium speed. Scrape down the bowl. Add the peanut butter and vanilla, and beat until combined. Fold in half of the whipped cream gently but thoroughly, then fold in the remaining whipped cream until completely combined.
4. Spoon the filling into the frozen crust, spreading it evenly. Cover the pie and refrigerate it for 2 hours.

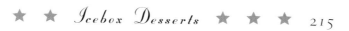

5. In a ceramic or glass bowl covered with plastic wrap, heat the chocolate chips with the cream on High in a microwave oven for 30-second intervals, stirring after each interval, until smooth.

Finish the pie:

6. Sprinkle the peanuts over the filling, then drizzle the chocolate cream over the pie. Chill for 2 more hours before serving.

Chocolate Candy Mud Pie

⇒ *Makes 12 servings* ⇐

*C*hocolate, cream cheese, and sour cream in a pecan crust with candy on top! That tells you what goes into this rich, rich, rich icebox pie, but it in no way conveys the beauty of all the textures at play here. You'll want to serve this in thin slices, with just-brewed espresso for the adults and frosty cold milk for the kids.

⇒ *Equipment Needed:* ★ 9-INCH DEEP-DISH PIE PAN ★ ELECTRIC MIXER

❦ Crust:

1½ cups all-purpose flour

½ teaspoon salt

8 tablespoons (1 stick) cold unsalted butter, cut into chunks

¾ cup finely chopped pecans, toasted

3 to 4 tablespoons ice water

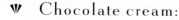 Filling:

12 ounces cream cheese, softened

1 cup sour cream

1½ cups powdered sugar

6 ounces semisweet chocolate, melted

1 tablespoon pure vanilla extract

6 ounces semisweet chocolate, chopped

✦ Chocolate cream:

4 ounces semisweet chocolate, coarsely
chopped

2 tablespoons heavy cream

✦ Garnish:

½ cup chocolate-covered toffee bits

Make the crust:

1. In a bowl, whisk together the flour and salt. With a pastry cutter, cut in the butter until the mixture is coarsely textured with small, irregular flakes and bits the size of small peas. Stir in the pecans until combined. Sprinkle on the water, 1 tablespoon at a time, stirring with a fork until the dough just holds together. Press the crust over the bottom and up the sides of the pie plate and freeze the shell for 20 minutes.

2. Preheat the oven to 375 degrees F.

3. Prick the chilled shell all over with the tines of a fork and bake for 18 minutes. Remove from the oven to a wire rack to cool.

Make the filling:

4. Put the cream cheese and sour cream in a bowl and beat until smooth using the electric mixer at medium speed. Scrape down the bowl. Add the powdered sugar and beat until combined. Add the melted chocolate and vanilla, and beat until smooth. Add the chopped chocolate and stir in using the mixer on low speed.

Make the chocolate cream:

5. In a ceramic or glass bowl covered with plastic wrap, heat the chocolate with the cream on High in a microwave oven for 30-second intervals, stirring after each interval until smooth.

Assemble the pie:

6. Pour the chocolate cream into the prebaked crust and spread it evenly. Place the filling on the crust and smooth the top. Garnish the pie with the toffee bits, arranging them in a circle around the edge of the pie. Refrigerate the pie for 2 hours before serving.

Debbi's Fudge Mousse

➤ *Makes 12 servings* ◄

An original American dessert it is not, but chocolate mousse has been adopted by Americans as if it had been invented and perfected here! The French word *mousse* means froth or foam, and describes what the texture of this ever-popular dessert should be. When made right, chocolate mousse can be like breathing in rich sweetened chocolate air. The airy texture sometimes comes from beaten egg whites or from softly whipped cream. In this version, it's the result of whole eggs beaten to three times their volume, then lightened with whipped cream. Take the time to really beat the eggs.

Use the best-quality chocolate you can find for this dessert. The better the chocolate, the better the flavor.

➤ *Equipment Needed:* ★ 8-INCH SPRINGFORM PAN ★ ELECTRIC MIXER

8 tablespoons (1 stick) unsalted butter, cut into chunks

8 ounces semisweet chocolate, coarsely chopped

2 tablespoons dark rum

1 tablespoon pure vanilla extract

1 tablespoon instant coffee crystals

3 large eggs

2 cups heavy cream, well chilled

1/2 cup powdered sugar

1/2 cup finely ground toasted pecans

Sliced strawberries, for garnish

Whipped cream, for garnish

1. Line the springform pan with plastic wrap, allowing the ends of the wrap to extend over the sides of the pan.
2. In a heavy-bottomed saucepan over low heat, melt the butter with the chocolate, stirring until smooth. Add the rum, vanilla, and coffee crystals, and stir until the crystals dissolve. Remove the pan from the heat.
3. Set a medium-size stainless-steel bowl over a pan of barely simmering water. Add the eggs and beat them until frothy using the electric mixer on medium speed. Increase the speed to high and beat until the eggs are hot and approximately triple in volume, about 5 minutes.
4. Gently fold the chocolate mixture into the eggs until no streaks remain. Remove from heat.
5. Put the cream and sugar in a chilled bowl and beat until thickened using the electric mixer and chilled beaters. Fold the cream into the chocolate mixture along with the pecans until fully combined.
6. Place the mousse in the prepared pan, cover with aluminum foil, and chill until very cold, about 4 hours, or overnight.
7. To serve, remove the sides of the springform pan and invert the mousse onto a serving plate. Remove the bottom of the pan and the plastic wrap. Cut into slices and garnish each slice with sliced strawberries and a dollop of whipped cream.

Chocolate Mousse Ring with Raspberry Whipped Cream

➤ *Makes 12 servings* ◄

This elegant dessert is smooth and incredibly rich, with texture more like a chocolate terrine than a French mousse that has been lightened with whipped cream or egg white.

The raspberry whipped cream makes the perfect accompaniment. If you like, fold the raspberry jam along with a few fresh berries into the whipped cream as well. You won't be able to pipe the cream then, but a slice of this, with a dollop of berry-filled cream on the side, makes a lovely individual serving.

➤ *Equipment Needed:* ★ 2-QUART RING MOLD ★ BAKING PAN ★ FOOD PROCESSOR ★ ELECTRIC MIXER ★ PASTRY BAG WITH #6 TIP

1¼ cups semisweet chocolate chips	2 tablespoons orange-flavored liqueur
1 cup sugar	2 teaspoons pure vanilla extract
½ cup boiling water	¼ teaspoon salt
4 large eggs	16 tablespoons (2 sticks) unsalted butter, softened

Ⱳ Raspberry cream:

1 cup heavy cream, well chilled	2 teaspoons pure vanilla extract
2 tablespoons sugar	4 tablespoons seedless red raspberry jam

Ⱳ Garnish:

Fresh raspberries

1. Preheat the oven to 350 degrees F. Butter the mold well. Have ready a baking pan large enough to hold the mold.

2. In the food processor, combine the chocolate chips, sugar, and boiling water until smooth. Add the eggs, liqueur, vanilla, and salt, and process until blended. Add half of the butter and process until smooth. Repeat with the remaining butter. Pour the mixture into the prepared mold, then carefully put it into the larger baking pan. Pour enough hot water into the baking pan to measure 2 inches.

3. Bake the mold for 50 to 55 minutes, or until firm to the touch and a skewer inserted in the center comes out clean. Remove the mold from the baking pan to a wire rack to cool for 30 minutes. Invert it onto a serving plate and let it set for 5 minutes before removing the mold. Cover with plastic wrap and chill for 2 hours.

Make the raspberry whipped cream:

4. Put the cream, sugar, and vanilla in a chilled bowl and beat on medium speed until thickened using the electric mixer and chilled beaters. Fold in the jam. Transfer some of the whipped cream to a pastry bag fitted with a decorative tip.

5. To serve, pipe a ribbon of whipped cream all around the mold and garnish the top with fresh raspberries. Cut the mousse into thin slices and garnish with additional raspberry cream, if desired.

Chapter 10

Kids' Corner

I LOVE BAKING WITH MY five daughters. It's a learning experience for them. For example, they learned fractions from measuring. They also like to try what they make, and are more likely to try new foods if they're involved in the cooking process. It's something we do for fun together, and I never hesitate to ask their opinions about recipes in the works—which icing on a cake tastes better than another or which brownie is absolutely their favorite of all. It was just that question which led to the first recipe in this group: Jennifer's Incredible Brownie Bites. When you turn to the recipe, you'll see that it has no nuts, an important feature for Jennifer (and a lot of other kids I know, too), and a wonderful topping that includes chocolate chips. Jennifer needed very little guidance from me in putting the ingredients together. It made me exceptionally proud to think that during all our fun times together baking she had been quietly learning. It was Jennifer who decided to cut her brownies into the size for small hands and small mouths.

The remaining recipes in the chapter, Oatmeal Cookie Pops, Fudge Dominoes, and Classic Caramel Apples are kid-friendly both tastewise and from a production point of view. Decorating the oatmeal cookies on popsicle sticks could be an activity at a youngster's birthday party or even at a Halloween fair.

As for the no-bake fudge dominoes, make them with your children on a rainy day when you have enough time to chill each layer of chocolate. You'll need the better part of the afternoon.

I remember absolutely loving caramel apples when I was a child. And I also remember how sticky my sisters and I were after eating them! For all you parents out there, it might be a good idea to make sure your kids are wearing smocks when you serve the caramel apples.

Fun to eat and fun to serve, these recipes are perfect family fare.

Jennifer's Incredible Brownie Bites

⇒ *Makes 36 brownies* ⇐

*A*ll my daughters love to help me out in the kitchen, and one day Jennifer, my fourteen-year-old, put these together almost by herself. You won't find any nuts in these brownies, but there's a lot of crunch and plenty of sweetness from a wonderful caramel and chocolate chip topping. Cutting these into bite-size pieces makes them all the more appealing. These brownies have never lasted past the day they were made.

⇒ *Equipment Needed:* ★ 9-INCH BAKING PAN ★ ELECTRIC MIXER

16 tablespoons (2 sticks) unsalted butter	1¼ cups all-purpose flour
¾ cup unsweetened cocoa powder	¼ teaspoon baking soda
4 large eggs, at room temperature	¼ teaspoon salt
1¾ cups sugar	¾ cup jarred caramel sauce
2 teaspoons pure vanilla extract	1 cup milk chocolate chips

1. Preheat the oven to 325 degrees F. Butter the baking pan, line it with aluminum foil, and butter the foil.

2. In a ceramic or glass bowl, melt the butter on Medium in a microwave oven for 30-second intervals. Stir the cocoa into the melted butter until smooth.

3. Put the eggs in a bowl and beat until frothy using an electric mixer on high speed. Slowly beat in the sugar. The mixture will be grainy. Add the butter mixture and vanilla and beat on low speed until thoroughly combined.

4. In a medium-size bowl, whisk together the flour, baking soda, and salt. Add the flour mixture to the butter mixture and beat until combined. Pour the batter into the prepared baking pan.

5. Bake for 30 to 35 minutes, or until a toothpick inserted in the center comes out with a few moist crumbs. The center should no longer be runny, but it will be soft when gently pressed with your fingertip. Remove the pan to a wire rack and let cool.

6. In a ceramic or glass bowl covered with plastic wrap, heat the caramel sauce on Medium in a microwave oven until spreadable. Pour it over the brownies, spreading it smooth with a rubber spatula. Sprinkle the chocolate chips evenly over the sauce. Chill the brownies for 1 hour to set.

7. To serve, cut the brownies into 1½-inch squares and watch them disappear!

Oatmeal Cookie Pops

Makes 18 cookie pops

*U*se this easy oatmeal cookie to introduce your children to baking. The batter is simple to put together, and turning the cookies into popsicles makes it more fun still. I like to make these with the girls at Halloween and decorate them with just orange and dark chocolate candies. If they last long enough, we give them out to trick-or-treaters.

But don't feel you have to decorate these cookies to enjoy them; they're very good oatmeal cookies just as is. They're a perfect lunchbox cookie, too.

Equipment Needed: ★ COOKIE SHEET ★ 18 WOODEN POPSICLE STICKS

2½ cups old-fashioned oats (see Tip, page 227)

2 cups all-purpose flour

2 teaspoons baking powder

½ teaspoon baking soda

1 teaspoon ground cinnamon

¼ teaspoon ground nutmeg

¼ teaspoon salt

16 tablespoons (2 sticks) unsalted butter, softened

1 cup firmly packed light brown sugar

¼ cup white sugar, plus additional for shaping

2 large eggs

2 tablespoons milk

▼ Finishing touches:

3 to 4 teaspoons milk

1 cup powdered sugar

½ cup creamy peanut butter

Assorted candies, for decoration

1. In a bowl, whisk together the oats, flour, baking powder, baking soda, cinnamon, nutmeg, and salt.
2. By hand or with electric mixer, cream together the butter and brown and white sugars in a large bowl until light and fluffy. Add the eggs and milk, and combine well. Add the oat mixture and stir until combined. Cover the bowl with plastic wrap and chill for 2 hours.
3. Preheat the oven to 300 degrees F.

4. Form the chilled dough into 1½-inch balls and place them 3 inches apart on a cookie sheet. Insert a popsicle stick into the side of each ball. Using the bottom of a glass dipped in white sugar, flatten each ball into a 2½-inch round.

5. Bake the cookies for 18 to 20 minutes, until the edges are golden brown. Remove from the oven and let the pops cool on a wire rack for 1 minute. Remove the pops to the racks to cool completely before decorating.

Prepare the finishing touches:

6. In a bowl, add milk to the powdered sugar until it is of easy spreading consistency. Make fun designs or faces with the icing and use the peanut butter as "glue" to stick the candies on the cookies.

➤ *Tip:* TYPES OF OATS

There are three basic types of oats at the supermarket: old-fashioned, quick, and instant. Old-fashioned oats are the least processed and take the longest time to cook. Neither quick nor instant oats can be substituted in this recipe.

Fudge Dominoes

➤ *Makes about 24 pieces* ≼

A microwave oven makes putting this recipe together a breeze, but you can also melt the chocolate on top of the stove. It's so pretty with its middle white layer, and kids love pushing the white chocolate chips on for the domino dots.

You need to store this fudge in the refrigerator, but for best flavor eat it at room temperature. For stovetop directions, see the Tip that follows the recipe.

➤ *Equipment Needed:* ★ 8-INCH SQUARE BAKING DISH

8 ounces semisweet chocolate, finely
  chopped
8 ounces milk chocolate, finely chopped
14 ounces sweetened condensed milk
2 tablespoons unsalted butter

1 teaspoon pure vanilla extract
½ cup heavy cream
12 ounces white chocolate, chopped
Miniature white chocolate chips as
  needed

1. Line the baking dish with aluminum foil and spray the foil with nonstick cooking spray.
2. In a ceramic or glass bowl covered with plastic wrap, heat the semisweet and milk chocolates on High in a microwave oven for 20-second intervals, stirring after each interval. Remove to a rack.
3. In another ceramic or glass bowl covered with plastic wrap, heat the milk and butter on High in a microwave oven for 45 seconds, until hot. Pour the hot milk mixture over the melted chocolate, add the vanilla, and with a rubber spatula combine until smooth.

4. Pour half of the mixture into the prepared baking dish, pressing it into the corners and smoothing the top. Put the dish in the freezer. Cover the remaining chocolate mixture and set aside.

5. In another microwave-safe bowl, heat the cream on High in the microwave in 30-second intervals until hot. You may need 2 or 3 intervals, and be careful because if overheated the cream will boil over. Pour the hot cream over the chopped white chocolate in a bowl and stir with a small wire whisk until smooth.

6. Remove the baking dish from the freezer and pour the white chocolate mixture over the chocolate layer, pressing it into the corners and smoothing it. Put the dish back in the freezer for 30 minutes.

7. Reheat the reserved chocolate mixture in the microwave until warm. Stir lightly, then pour over the chilled white chocolate layer in the baking dish. As before, press it into the corners, using a metal spatula. Cover with aluminum foil and put it in the refrigerator for 1 hour.

8. With a small, sharp knife, cut the fudge into domino-sized rectangles and press chips into the fudge, pointed side down, creating the dots on a domino.

9. Keep the fudge, covered, in the refrigerator, but for the best flavor, eat it at room temperature.

➢ *Tip:* STOVETOP DIRECTIONS FOR FUDGE DOMINOES

To make this recipe on the stovetop, heat the condensed milk and butter in a heavy-bottomed saucepan. Pour the hot mixture over the semisweet and milk chocolates in a bowl, add the vanilla, and stir until smooth. Pour into the baking dish and freeze as directed in Step 4. In another heavy-bottomed saucepan, heat the cream, then pour it over the white chocolate in a bowl and stir until the chocolate is melted smooth. Layer the chocolate mixtures as directed.

Classic Caramel Apples

➤ *Makes 1 dozen dipped apples* ◄

*I*f caramel apples are good, why wouldn't caramel-dipped chocolate-covered apples be even better? They are! Because these are so rich and sticky, take a pretty muffin liner cup—foil ones are especially nice, and sturdy besides—and push them up on the popsicle stick to catch the drips!

A crisp, firm apple is needed here. I like to use a few firm Golden Delicious apples in addition to the Granny Smiths and Macs. If you use McIntosh, be sure they're this year's crop.

➤ *Equipment Needed:* ★ 12 WOODEN POPSICLE STICKS

12 small red and green apples, such as Granny Smiths and McIntosh

30 ounces high-quality apple-dipping caramel (see Tip, page 231)

8 ounces white chocolate, chopped

8 ounces semisweet chocolate, chopped

1. Twist the stem off each apple and insert a popsicle stick into the stem end.
2. Prepare the dipping caramel according to the package directions. Dip the apples carefully, 1 at a time, into the prepared caramel, covering the surface. Place the apples on wax paper and let set for 30 minutes.
3. While the caramel is setting, in separate heavy saucepans (or in the microwave), melt the white chocolate and semisweet chocolate over low heat, stirring until smooth. Dip some of the apples in the white chocolate, letting the excess drip off. Place on wax paper and let them set in the freezer for 5 minutes. Dip the remaining apples in the dark chocolate and let them set in the freezer for 5 minutes. Then, if desired, dip the apples into the contrasting chocolate. Let the chocolate coverings harden in the refrigerator for about 30 minutes.

➤ *Tip:* Caramel Apple Dip

Look for caramel apple dip in the produce section of the supermarket. It comes in plastic tubs. If you're planning to make these more than once, do what I do: Buy a few tubs to keep in the pantry.

Chapter 11

Coffee Cakes and Muffins

I'M NOT SURE WHEN people started having something sweet with their breakfast, but there's no denying that coffee cakes, sweet breads, and muffins go beautifully with a cup of freshly brewed coffee in the morning. Just because we're busy and don't have as much time to bake as we used to doesn't mean we have to forgo a home-baked morning sweet altogether. These recipes are basically quick breads leavened with baking powder and/or baking soda.

What I really like about the two coffee cake recipes and the two muffin recipes in this section is that they aren't your everyday fare. Cinnamon Swirl Coffee Cake (page 234) has sour cream added to the batter, which makes it rich and fine, and a delicious pecan and brown sugar streusel topping. Then there's a very special coffee cake (page 236) that I like to make on holiday weekends or for a birthday breakfast. It's filled with mascarpone, Italy's lovely, rich double-cream cheese, and a few other goodies as well.

My version of the great American blueberry muffin (page 238) has an oat and sugar topping. And if you prefer a tangy flavor, I've mixed mandarin oranges with dried cranberries in a beautiful citrusy batter. Pair the Orange Blossom Muffins (page 240) with a glass of fresh orange juice. You won't believe the harmony of flavors.

Don't restrict yourself to eating these treats only in the morning. Serve them at teatime or pack a muffin or slice of the coffee cake into a lunchbox or snack pack for your kids—or yourself!

Cinnamon Swirl Coffee Cake

⋟ *Makes 12 servings* ⋞

I can't remember where it was, but I've never forgotten the taste of a simple cinnamony streusel-topped coffee cake I had as a child. In honor of that memory, I present this cake. It has a streusel topping, just like the one I've never been able to forget, that caramelizes a little when it's done, and a cinnamon-swirl throughout. Check your cinnamon—it should be fresh and filled with flavor—and if you can, be sure to serve this cake still warm from the oven, when it is at its absolute best.

⋟ *Equipment Needed:* ★ 10-INCH TUBE PAN ★ ELECTRIC MIXER

❦ Cake:

16 tablespoons (2 sticks) unsalted butter, softened

1 cup sugar

2 teaspoons pure vanilla extract

3 large eggs, at room temperature

2 cups all-purpose flour

½ teaspoon baking powder

½ teaspoon baking soda

Pinch of salt

½ cup sour cream

❦ Syrup:

2 tablespoons unsalted butter, melted

3 teaspoons sugar

1 teaspoon ground cinnamon

❦ Streusel:

1 cup firmly packed light brown sugar

2 teaspoons ground cinnamon

1 cup chopped pecans, toasted

8 tablespoons (1 stick) cold unsalted butter, cut
 into tablespoons

1. Preheat the oven to 350 degrees F. Butter and flour the tube pan.

Make the cake:

2. Put the butter and sugar in a bowl and cream together using the electric mixer on medium speed until fluffy, about 5 minutes. Scrape down the bowl. Add the vanilla and eggs, 1 at a time, beating for 20 seconds after each addition. Scrape down the bowl again.

3. In another bowl, whisk together the flour, baking powder, baking soda, and salt. Add this mixture to the butter mixture in thirds, alternating with the sour cream. Beat for 45 seconds after each addition, and begin and end with the flour mixture. Pour the batter into the prepared tube pan.

Make the syrup:

4. In a small bowl, stir together the melted butter, sugar, and cinnamon.
5. Drizzle the syrup over the batter and with the blade of a knife or a skewer, swirl the syrup through the batter.

Make the streusel:

6. In a bowl, combine the sugar, cinnamon, and pecans. With a pastry cutter, cut in the butter, a few pieces at a time, until the mixture resembles coarse crumbs. Scatter the streusel over the batter in the pan.

7. Bake for 50 to 55 minutes, or until a cake tester inserted in the center comes out clean. Remove the pan from the oven to a wire rack to cool for 15 minutes. Serve warm or at room temperature.

Creamy Cheese-Filled Coffee Cake

*W*e all know how wonderful a fresh-baked cheese Danish can be, so why not take that idea and work it into homemade coffee cake? Here it is, in all its delicious glory, and with a few extra touches. For the cheese I've used Italy's rich and buttery mascarpone, which is available in specialty food stores. If you can't find it, simply substitute good old-fashioned American cream cheese. A pecan topping adds crunch to this buttery, moist, pound cake–type crumb, and if you feel like going all out, drizzle it with chocolate cream. Glazed or plain, this makes a wonderful brunch or holiday breakfast or even tea cake. And it freezes well, too.

➤ *Equipment Needed:*   ★   10-INCH SPRINGFORM PAN   ★   ELECTRIC MIXER

❦ Cake:

16 tablespoons (2 sticks) unsalted butter, softened

1 cup sugar

2 teaspoons pure vanilla extract

3 large eggs, at room temperature

2 cups all-purpose flour

$\frac{1}{2}$ teaspoon baking powder

$\frac{1}{2}$ teaspoon baking soda

$\frac{1}{2}$ teaspoon salt

$\frac{1}{2}$ cup sour cream

❦ Cheese filling:

8 ounces mascarpone cheese, at room temperature

$\frac{1}{4}$ cup sugar

1 large egg, at room temperature

1 teaspoon pure vanilla extract

$\frac{1}{2}$ cup raspberry preserves, as accompaniment

❦ Nut topping:

$\frac{1}{2}$ cup all-purpose flour

2 tablespoons firmly packed light brown sugar

$\frac{1}{4}$ teaspoon salt

$\frac{1}{2}$ cup chopped pecans, toasted

4 tablespoons ($\frac{1}{2}$ stick) unsalted butter, melted

♥ Chocolate drizzle (optional):

1 ounce semisweet chocolate   *3 tablespoons heavy cream*

1. Preheat the oven to 350 degrees F. Butter the springform pan.

Make the cake:

2. Put the butter and sugar in a bowl and cream together using the electric mixer on medium speed until fluffy, about 5 minutes. Scrape down the bowl. Add the vanilla and eggs, 1 at a time, beating for 20 seconds after each addition. Scrape down the bowl again.
3. In another bowl, whisk together the flour, baking powder, baking soda, and salt. Add this mixture to the butter mixture in thirds, alternating with the sour cream. Beat for 45 seconds after each addition, and begin and end with the flour mixture. Spread the batter in the prepared pan.

Make the cheese filling:

4. Put the mascarpone and sugar in a bowl and beat until smooth, 2 to 3 minutes, using the electric mixer on medium speed. Add the egg and vanilla, and beat until blended. Pour the filling over the center of the batter in the pan, leaving a 1-inch border all the way around.
5. In a microwave-safe bowl covered with plastic wrap, heat the raspberry preserves on High in a microwave oven until pourable. Pour evenly over the cheese filling.

Make the nut topping:

6. In a small bowl, whisk together the flour, sugar, and salt. Add the pecans and combine. Stir in the butter until the dry ingredients are moistened. Sprinkle the nut topping evenly over the batter.
7. Bake for 55 to 60 minutes, until the top is golden brown; the center will still be jiggly. Remove the cake to a wire rack and let cool for 1 hour in the pan. Run a thin knife around the sides of the pan to loosen the cake and remove the sides of the pan. Serve the cake as is or prepare the chocolate drizzle.

Prepare the drizzle:

8. In a ceramic or glass bowl covered with plastic wrap, heat the chocolate with the cream on High in a microwave oven for 30-second intervals, stirring after each interval, until smooth. (It should take 40–60 seconds, total.)
9. Drizzle the hot chocolate cream from the tines of a fork over the cake. Transfer the cake to a serving plate and serve in slices.

Debbi's Blueberry Muffins

⋟ *Makes 1 dozen* ⋞

I've always loved homemade blueberry muffins, and it was only a matter of time before I figured out how to combine their buttery moistness with a crunchy oat and brown sugar topping for an incredible contrast in textures and tastes.

These muffins freeze beautifully, so you can always have a batch on hand. To thaw, transfer them to the refrigerator the night before you want to serve them. All you have to do in the morning is pop them in a Warm oven for 15 minutes, then see if your family doesn't jump out of bed! Besides being a breakfast treat, these make a great lunchbox or after-school snack.

⋟ *Equipment Needed:* ★ 12-CUP MUFFIN PAN (OR TWO 6-CUP PANS)

2¾ cups all-purpose flour

¾ cup white sugar

¾ cup firmly packed light brown sugar

1 teaspoon baking powder

1 teaspoon baking soda

½ teaspoon salt

2 large eggs, at room temperature, lightly beaten

12 tablespoons (1½ sticks) unsalted butter, melted

¾ cup buttermilk

1 tablespoon pure vanilla extract

1½ teaspoons pure lemon extract

1 cup frozen unsweetened blueberries (see Tip, page 239)

❦ Topping:

¾ cup old-fashioned or quick-cooking oats (not instant, see Tip: Types of Oats, page 227)

¼ cup white sugar

¼ cup firmly packed light brown sugar

4 tablespoons (½ stick) unsalted butter, melted

1. Preheat the oven to 375 degrees. Press a paper liner into each muffin cup, then spray the top of the muffin pan with nonstick cooking spray.

2. In a large bowl, whisk together the flour, white and brown sugars, baking powder, baking soda, and salt.

3. In another bowl, combine well the eggs, melted butter, buttermilk, and vanilla and lemon extracts. Add this mixture to the dry ingredients, folding it in only until the flour is incorporated. (Overbeating the batter will make the muffins tough.) Fold in the blueberries gently.

4. With an ice-cream scoop or a ½-cup measure, drop batter into each prepared muffin cup, mounding it slightly in the center.

Make the topping:

5. In a bowl, combine the oatmeal and white and brown sugars. Add the melted butter and stir to moisten.

6. Spoon 1 tablespoon of the topping onto each muffin, lightly pressing it in with your fingertips.

7. Bake for 20 to 25 minutes, or until a cake tester inserted in the center of a muffin comes out clean. Remove the pan to a wire rack and let cool for 10 minutes, then take the muffins out of the pan and let cool completely on the rack.

➤ Tip: FREEZING BLUEBERRIES

The blueberries are best added to the batter when they're still semi-frozen because semi-solid berries retain their shape more successfully than thawed ones. If you remove the berries from the freezer to thaw slightly on a plate about 30 minutes before you expect to add them to the batter, they should bake up beautifully.

You can also freeze your own berries. Buy fresh berries when they're in season. Wash and drain them. Arrange them in a single layer on a baking sheet and put the sheet in the freezer. When frozen hard, put the berries in plastic bags and store in the freezer. By freezing them individually, you'll be able, in the future, to measure out only as many as you need.

Orange Blossom Muffins

My thinking went like this: If cranberry-orange quick bread is good, wouldn't muffins made with mandarin oranges and dried cranberries be great? They are. And you can make these in a moment's notice because if your pantry shelves are well stocked, you'll have both of the main ingredients on hand. Piled up in a pretty basket and wrapped in colorful paper and ribbon, these make a beautiful gift any time of year.

I like to serve these for breakfast or brunch, but they're also very good with dinner, as an accompaniment to a roast turkey or an old-fashioned stew. Remember that the secret to tender muffins is not to overmix the batter. And if you want them more orangey still, add freshly grated orange peel.

➤ *Equipment Needed:* ★ 12-CUP MUFFIN PAN

2¾ cups all-purpose flour

¾ cup firmly packed light brown sugar

¾ cup white sugar, plus an additional 2 tablespoons for sprinkling

1 teaspoon baking powder

1 teaspoon baking soda

½ teaspoon salt

12 tablespoons (1½ sticks) unsalted butter, melted

2 large eggs, at room temperature, lightly beaten

¾ cup buttermilk

1 tablespoon pure vanilla extract

¾ teaspoon pure lemon extract

¾ teaspoon pure orange extract

¾ cup coarsely chopped mandarin orange segments, drained

¾ cup dried sweetened cranberries

1. Preheat the oven to 375 degrees F. Press a paper liner into each muffin cup, then spray the top of the muffin pan with nonstick cooking spray.
2. In a large bowl, whisk together the flour, brown sugar, ¾ cup white sugar, baking powder, baking soda, and salt.
3. In a medium bowl, combine the melted butter, eggs, buttermilk, and vanilla, lemon, and orange extracts. Add this mixture to the dry ingredients, folding it in only until the flour is incorporated. Overbeating the batter will make the muffins tough. Fold in the orange segments and dried cranberries.

4. With an ice-cream scoop or ½-cup measure, drop batter into each prepared muffin cup, mounding it slightly in the center. Sprinkle the top of each muffin with ½ teaspoon of the remaining white sugar.

5. Bake the muffins for 20 to 25 minutes, or until a toothpick inserted in the center comes out clean. Remove the muffin pan to a wire rack and let the muffins cool for 10 minutes, then take them out of the pan and let cool completely on the rack.

Chapter 12

Pound Cakes and Bundt Cakes

As much as I love fancy cakes loaded with fillings and frostings, I have a special place in my heart for pound cake.

The original recipe for pound cake was even simpler than it is today. It was made by weight (hence the name, *pound* cake), with four ingredients: one pound of flour, one pound of butter, one pound of eggs, and one pound of sugar. A recipe doesn't get much easier to remember than that!

Over the years, the proportions of the classic pound cake have changed and other ingredients have been added, but an old-fashioned pound cake and a new-fashioned one share one very important feature: a delicious dense crumb. I've added finely chopped almonds to my favorite pound cake recipe on page 244 and included a lemony rum sauce for serving with it, too. Sauced or not, it's the type of cake that can be served for dessert or with tea or even for breakfast (without sauce, of course!). I like to bake my pound cakes in a bundt pan.

A close relative of pound cake is the bundt cake. Baked in a distinctive pan, bundt cakes stand tall and stately and have a similar dense crumb and comforting texture. I find their rich simplicity enormously appealing and have included three versions here. Serve the first, Mandarin Orange Pound Cake (page 246), either for dessert or for breakfast, but the remaining three cakes—espresso, glazed chocolate, and white chocolate, should be reserved for dessert or perhaps for a formal tea.

Around the holidays, Christmas and New Year's, in addition to all the cookies my daughters and I bake, there's always a pound cake, a bundt cake, or both on hand. It's what we serve when friends stop by or what we take to a potluck supper. There's tradition behind these kinds of cakes—the lovely tradition of serving something that looks and says home-baked.

Debbi's Pound Cake

*I*ngredients such as sour cream, buttermilk, and butter guarantee a tender crumb, which is what this wonderful cake has. I couldn't resist adding some chopped toasted almonds in the batter and a rum and lemon sauce as well. The sauce is optional but nice if you feel like dressing this up. Raspberry Sauce (see page 77) is also tasty with this old-fashioned favorite, as is a little raspberry jam spread on a toasted slice in the morning.

⇒ *Equipment Needed:* ★ 10-INCH 3-QUART BUNDT PAN ★ ELECTRIC MIXER

❦ Cake:

3 cups sifted all-purpose flour

½ teaspoon baking soda

½ teaspoons salt

16 tablespoons (2 sticks) unsalted butter, softened, plus 1 tablespoon for buttering the pan

2 cups sugar, plus 2 tablespoons for sugaring the pan

2 teaspoons pure vanilla extract

2 teaspoons pure lemon extract

4 large eggs, at room temperature, separated

½ cup buttermilk

⅓ cup sour cream

1 cup finely chopped almonds, toasted

❦ Rum and lemon sauce:

4 tablespoons (½ stick) unsalted butter

½ cup heavy cream

½ cup packed dark brown sugar

¼ teaspoon salt

3 tablespoons dark rum

3 tablespoons fresh lemon juice

1. Preheat the oven to 350 degrees F. Butter and sugar the pan.

Make the cake:

2. In a bowl, whisk together the flour, baking soda, and salt.
3. Put the butter and sugar in a large bowl and cream together until fluffy, 4 to 5 minutes, using the electric mixer on high speed. Add the vanilla and lemon extracts and egg yolks, 1 at a time, beating on low speed for 20 seconds after each addition. Scrape down the bowl.
4. In another bowl, combine the buttermilk and sour cream until smooth.
5. Beat the flour mixture in thirds into the butter mixture, alternating with the buttermilk mixture, beating 45 seconds after each addition. Stir in the almonds until combined.
6. Put the egg whites in another large bowl and beat until stiff peaks form using the mixer on high speed and clean beaters. Fold the beaten whites gently but thoroughly into the batter.
7. Pour the batter into the prepared pan and bake for 50 to 55 minutes. The top will be brown and still a little soft to the touch, and a toothpick inserted in the center will come out with a few crumbs sticking to it. Remove the cake to a wire rack to cool in the pan for 20 minutes, then turn it out on the rack to cool completely.

Make the rum and lemon sauce:

8. In a medium-size saucepan over medium heat, melt the butter. Add the cream, sugar, and salt, and bring to a boil, stirring to dissolve the sugar. Remove the pan from the heat and stir in the rum and lemon juice. Transfer the sauce to a serving bowl.

9. To serve, cut the cake into slices and serve the sauce alongside.

Mandarin Orange Pound Cake

➤ *Makes 12 servings* ◄

I've always loved to use mandarin oranges in breakfast cakes and muffins; their special sweetness seems to be the perfect start to a day. This pound cake, which I do serve for brunch (and tea and dessert, as well), is simple but rich and dense. It has lots of sweet butter and plenty of eggs, which give it a lovely golden color. A dusting of powdered sugar makes it especially pretty.

➤ *Equipment Needed:* ★ 10-INCH 3-QUART BUNDT PAN ★ ELECTRIC MIXER

3 cups all-purpose flour

1 teaspoon baking powder

$^1\!/_2$ teaspoon salt

24 tablespoons (3 sticks) unsalted butter, softened, plus 1 tablespoon for buttering the pan

2 cups sugar, plus 2 tablespoons for sugaring the pan

6 large egg yolks

2 teaspoons pure orange extract

1 teaspoon pure vanilla extract

1 tablespoon grated fresh orange peel (about 1 orange)

$^1\!/_2$ cup buttermilk

One 11-ounce can mandarin oranges, drained and lightly pressed in a sieve to remove excess juice; juice reserved

1 tablespoon orange liqueur

3 tablespoons powdered sugar, for garnish

1. Preheat the oven to 350 degrees F. Butter and sugar the bundt pan.

2. In a bowl, sift together the flour, baking powder, and salt.

3. Put the butter and sugar in a bowl and cream together using the electric mixer on high speed. Scrape down the bowl. Add the egg yolks, 2 at a time, beating for 20 seconds after each addition. Add the orange and vanilla extracts and orange peel, and beat using the mixer at low speed. Beat in the flour mixture in thirds, alternating with the buttermilk, beating for 45 seconds after each addition. Scrape down the bowl with a rubber spatula.

4. Add the mandarin oranges and beat on low speed until fully incorporated. Pour the batter into the prepared pan.

5. Bake for 55 to 65 minutes, or until a cake tester inserted in the center comes out clean. Remove the cake to a wire rack and cool for 10 minutes, then turn it out on the rack to cool to room temperature.

6. In a small, heavy saucepan over medium heat, reduce the reserved mandarin orange juice until thick and syrupy, about 3 tablespoons in all. Stir in the orange liqueur. Brush the glaze over the still-warm cake and let dry. Before serving, dust the cake with the powdered sugar.

Espresso Bundt Cake

*T*his rich, mocha-flavored bundt cake is unforgettable. The stronger the coffee you use, the better the mocha flavor. A slice of this, topped with a scoop of coffee ice cream and a drizzle of chocolate sauce, makes a very pleasing dessert.

⇒ *Equipment Needed:* ★ 10-INCH 3-QUART BUNDT PAN ★ ELECTRIC MIXER

❦ Cake:

1 tablespoon instant coffee crystals

¾ cup fresh-brewed hot espresso or other strong coffee

¼ cup coffee-flavored liqueur

1 tablespoon pure vanilla extract

24 tablespoons (3 sticks) unsalted butter, softened, plus 1 tablespoon for buttering the pan

2 cups sugar, plus 2 tablespoons for sugaring the pan

5 large eggs, at room temperature

3 ounces semisweet chocolate, melted (see How to Melt Chocolate, page 18)

3 cups all-purpose flour

1 teaspoon baking powder

½ teaspoon baking soda

½ teaspoon salt

2 tablespoons powdered sugar (optional)

❦ Glaze:

2 ounces semisweet chocolate, coarsely chopped

1 tablespoon unsalted butter

1 cup sifted powdered sugar

5 to 6 tablespoons espresso or other strong coffee

1. Preheat the oven to 350 degrees F. Butter and sugar the bundt pan.

Make the cake:

2. In a small saucepan, dissolve the coffee crystals in the hot coffee. Stir in the liqueur and vanilla. Set aside.
3. Put the butter and sugar in a bowl and cream together until fluffy using the electric mixer on medium speed. Add the eggs, 1 at a time, beating for 20 seconds after each addition. Scrape down the bowl. Add the melted chocolate and beat on low speed until combined. Scrape down the bowl again.
4. In a bowl, whisk together the flour, baking powder, baking soda, and salt. Add this mixture to the butter mixture in thirds, alternating with the coffee mixture. Beat for 45 seconds after each addition.
5. Scrape the batter into the prepared pan and bake for 55 to 60 minutes. The top will be soft, and a cake tester inserted in the center will come out with moist crumbs. Remove the cake to a wire rack to cool for 15 minutes. Invert the cake carefully onto a plate; turn the cake again, right side up, and let cool to room temperature. If desired, dust the cake lightly with powdered sugar before glazing.

Make the glaze:

6. While the cake bakes, in a ceramic or glass bowl covered with plastic wrap, heat the chocolate and butter in a microwave oven on High for 20-second intervals, stirring after each interval, until smooth. Add ½ cup sugar and 3 tablespoons coffee, and whisk until smooth. Slowly add the remaining sugar and coffee, and whisk until smooth.
7. Pierce the entire top of the cake with a thin skewer. Spoon or drizzle the glaze over the top.
8. To serve, transfer the cake to a serving plate and serve in slices.

Glazed Chocolate Bundt Cake

➢ *Makes 12 servings* ⬳

*L*ots of chocolate flavor and a gorgeous texture make this bundt cake very special. Texture is essential. The more you beat the batter, the more velvety the crumb. I like to serve this cake for dessert in the summer with raspberries and a little Raspberry Sauce (see page 77). I added a brandy-scented sugar glaze below, but chocolate glaze (see page 248) would be nice, too.

➢ *Equipment Needed:* ★ 10-INCH 3-QUART BUNDT PAN ★ ELECTRIC MIXER

❦ Cake:

6 ounces unsweetened chocolate

16 tablespoons (2 sticks) unsalted butter, softened, plus 1 tablespoon for buttering the pan

3 cups sugar, plus 2 tablespoons for sugaring the pan

1 tablespoon pure vanilla extract

1 teaspoon pure orange extract (optional)

2 tablespoons grated fresh orange peel (optional)

6 large eggs, at room temperature

3 cups all-purpose flour

1 teaspoon baking powder

$1/4$ teaspoon baking soda

$1/4$ teaspoon salt

$3/4$ cup sour cream

2 tablespoons powdered sugar (optional)

❦ Glaze:

3 tablespoons brandy

1 tablespoon pure vanilla extract

2 tablespoons unsalted butter

$1^1/2$ cups powdered sugar

1. Preheat the oven to 350 degrees F. Butter and sugar the bundt pan.

Make the cake:

2. In a ceramic or glass bowl covered with plastic wrap, heat the chocolate on High in a microwave oven for 30-second intervals, stirring after each interval, until smooth.

3. Put the butter and sugar in a bowl and cream together until fluffy using the electric mixer on medium speed. Add the vanilla and orange extracts and orange peel, if using, and beat until combined. Add the eggs, 1 at a time, beating for 20 seconds after each addition. Scrape down the bowl. Beat in the warm chocolate.

4. In a bowl, sift together the flour, baking powder, baking soda, and salt. Add the flour mixture to the butter mixture in thirds, alternating with the sour cream. Beat for 45 seconds after each addition. Scrape down the bowl. Scrape the batter into the prepared pan and smooth the top.

5. Bake for 55 to 60 minutes. The top of the cake will feel soft when pressed, and a cake tester inserted in the center will come out moist. Remove the cake to a wire rack to cool for 15 minutes, then turn it out of the pan and cool to room temperature. If desired, dust the cake lightly with powdered sugar before glazing.

Make the glaze:

6. In a saucepan, warm the brandy and vanilla over low heat, then stir in the butter until melted. Remove the pan from the heat and stir in the powdered sugar until smooth.

7. Place the cake on a serving plate and spoon the glaze over it. Or slice the cake and spoon glaze over each serving.

White Chocolate Bundt Cake

≥ *Makes 12 servings* ≤

*I*f dark chocolate bundt cake is special, how about this white chocolate version! It's buttery and very rich, studded with pieces of white chocolate throughout. The glaze uses both dark and white chocolates in a beautiful contrast.

     An important shopping tip: Please use the highest quality—meaning imported—white chocolate here. Read the label: You'll be able to determine the quality by the percentage of cocoa butter. The higher the percentage, the better the quality. As for quantity, you'll need one pound!

≥ *Equipment Needed:*   ★   10-INCH, 3-QUART CAPACITY BUNDT PAN
          ★   ELECTRIC MIXER   ★   SQUEEZE BOTTLE

❦ Cake:

3 cups all-purpose flour

1 teaspoon baking powder

1/4 teaspoon baking soda

1/2 teaspoon salt

16 tablespoons (2 sticks) unsalted butter, softened, plus 1 tablespoon for buttering the pan

2 cups sugar, plus 2 tablespoons for sugaring the pan

1 1/2 teaspoons pure vanilla extract

1/2 teaspoon pure almond extract

5 large eggs, at room temperature

4 ounces white chocolate, melted and still warm

1 cup sour cream

4 ounces white chocolate chunks or chips

❦ White chocolate ganache:

8 ounces white chocolate, coarsely chopped

1/2 cup heavy cream

4 ounces semisweet chocolate, melted and still warm

1. Preheat the oven to 350 degrees F. Butter and sugar the bundt pan.

Make the cake:

2. In a bowl, sift together the flour, baking powder, baking soda, and salt.
3. Put the butter and sugar in a bowl and cream together using the electric mixer on medium speed until light and fluffy. Add the vanilla and almond extracts and the eggs, 1 at a time, beating for 20 seconds after each addition. Slowly beat in the melted chocolate. Scrape down the bowl.
4. Add the flour mixture to the butter mixture in thirds, alternating with the sour cream. Beat for 45 seconds after each addition. Place the batter in the prepared pan in 3 layers, separating each layer with chocolate chunks or chips.

5. Bake for 55 to 60 minutes. The top will be brown, and a cake tester inserted in the center will come out with a few crumbs on it. Remove the cake to a wire rack to cool for 15 minutes, then invert it onto the wire rack and let cool to room temperature.

Make the white chocolate ganache:

6. In a ceramic or glass bowl covered with plastic wrap, heat the white chocolate with the heavy cream on High in a microwave oven for 30-second intervals, stirring after each interval, until smooth. Let the ganache cool for about 10 minutes, then drizzle it over the cake in a decorative pattern.
7. Pour the melted semisweet chocolate into the squeeze bottle and squeeze it over the white chocolate in a decorative pattern.
8. Transfer the cake to a serving plate.

Liquid and Dry Measure Equivalents

American	Metric
¼ TEASPOON	1.25 MILLILITERS
½ TEASPOON	2.5 MILLILITERS
1 TEASPOON	5 MILLILITERS
1 TABLESPOON	15 MILLILITERS
1 FLUID OUNCE	30 MILLILITERS
¼ CUP	60 MILLILITERS
⅓ CUP	80 MILLILITERS
½ CUP	120 MILLILITERS
1 CUP	240 MILLILITERS
1 PINT (2 CUPS)	480 MILLILITERS
1 QUART (4 CUPS; 32 OUNCES)	960 MILLILITERS (.96 LITER)
1 GALLON (4 QUARTS)	3.84 LITERS
1 OUNCE (BY WEIGHT)	28 GRAMS
¼ POUND (4 OUNCES)	114 GRAMS
1 POUND (16 OUNCES)	454 GRAMS
2.2 POUNDS	1 KILOGRAM (1,000 GRAMS)

Oven Temperature Equivalents

Description	Fahrenheit	Celsius
COOL	200	90
VERY SLOW	250	120
SLOW	300–325	150–160
MODERATELY SLOW	325–350	160–180
MODERATE	350–375	180–190
MODERATELY HOT	375–400	190–200
HOT	400–450	200–230
VERY HOT	450–500	230–260

INDEX